A Child's First Library of Learning

Science Starter

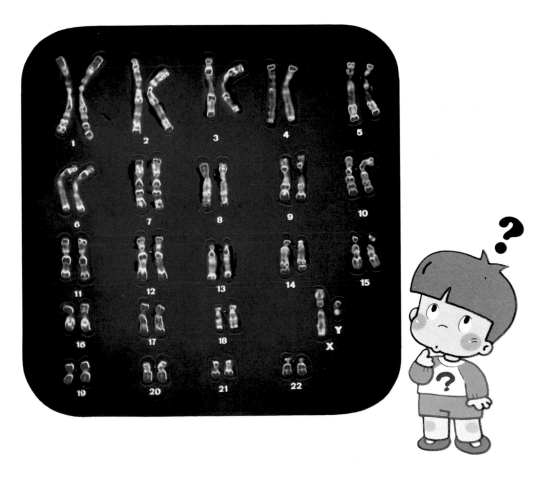

TIME-LIFE BOOKS • ALEXANDRIA, VIRGINIA

Contents

What Is It Like Inside the Earth?...4

Why Does a Compass Point North?..6

What Kind of Material Are the Earth and Planets Made Of?.....................8

How Is the Size of the Earth Measured?..10

How Were the Oceans Made?...12

What Is the Ocean Floor Like?...14

Did You Know That Oceans Flow?..16

How Are Lakes Made?...18

How Are Rocks Formed?...20

How Is Oil Made? 22

How Is Coal Formed?...24

How Are Limestone Caves Made?..26

How Does a Geyser Shoot Water So High Into the Air?.........................28

How High Does the Atmosphere Go?...30

Why Does a Low-Pressure Area Usually Bring Rain?............................32

How Does a Tornado Start?...34

What Causes a Glacier?...36

Why Do We See a Mirage When Nothing Is There? 38

How and When Did the Universe Start?...40

What Makes an Eclipse of the Moon?..42

How Far Away Are the Stars?..44

Why Do People Float Inside a Spaceship?......................................46

How Many Colors Does Sunlight Have?......................................48

Why Is Some Smoke Black But Other Smoke Is Gray or White?......................50

Why Can't We See a Smell?......................................52

Why Does a Golf Ball Have Dimples?......................................54

Why Does a Tennis Ball Curve if It Is Hit With a Slicing Motion?......................56

How Do Fishing Boats Find Fish When the Ocean Is So Big?......................58

Why Don't Birds Get Shocked When They Sit on an Electric Wire?......................60

Why Does Food Spoil?......................................62

Did You Know That a Diamond Is the Hardest Stone?......................................64

Why Doesn't the World Run Out of Oxygen?......................................66

Why Does Ice Float in Water?......................................68

Why Doesn't Dry Ice Turn to Water the Way Regular Ice Does?......................70

How Is Uranium Used to Make Electricity?......................................72

How Do Farmers Grow Seedless Grapes?......................................74

How Is Glass Made?......................................76

What Are These?......................................78

And What Are These?......................................80

Growing-Up Album......................................81

What Is It Like Inside the Earth?

ANSWER The earth is made up of three parts, which can be compared to the parts of an apple. The apple's skin is like the earth's crust. The part we eat is like the earth's mantle, or heavy coat. Where we find the seeds is like the earth's core. The inside of the earth is not like jelly as people used to think.

Oute

Inner core

● **To the Parent**

The earth has three parts: a crust, mantle and core. The nature of the inside of the earth is determined from waves transmitted during earthquakes, which travel at different speeds under varying conditions. The mantle extends 1,800 miles (2,900 km) down from the crust. It is in constant flux, which causes endless shifting of the crustal plates. The outer core is molten, and the inner core may also be. Both are probably iron and nickel. Estimates of the core's temperature range from 4,000° to 8,000° F. (2,200° to 4,400° C.).

Mantle

Crust

The earth could also be
compared to an egg, with
the shell as the crust,
the white as the mantle
and the yolk as the core.

■ An uneven crust

The crust is as thick as 20 miles (35 km) beneath land
but only about 3 miles (5 km) thick under the oceans.

■ Mantle

Part of the mantle is
made of rock so hot
that it has melted.
This molten rock can
seep through cracks in
the crust and pour out
of volcanoes. It is
then called lava. When
fiery lava cools, it
turns hard as stone.

■ Core

Scientists believe
that the core of the
earth is made up of
very heavy metals like
iron and nickel. The
outer core is made of
molten rock. The inner
core might be liquid
too, but scientists
don't know for certain.

MINI-DATA

Ridge

Plate

Trench

Mantle

Molten rock in the mantle pushes through
the ocean floor and forms plates that
flow both ways. When plates meet, one
is pushed beneath the other, making
trenches and causing earthquakes.

Why Does a Compass Point North?

ANSWER The inside of the earth acts like a strong magnet. One end of the magnet is near the North Pole. The other end is near the South Pole. A compass has a needle that's a magnet. The earth's magnet attracts the needle so it always points north and south.

North Pole

South Pole

6

and S poles attract each other.

Magnetic force lines

• **To the Parent**

Scientists believe that the earth has a core of molten iron and nickel and that the earth's rotation turns the core into an electrical generator, producing a magnetic field. In effect, the earth acts as a magnet, with the magnet's ends near the north and south geographical poles. Lines of magnetic force between the two ends curve around the surface of the earth. A compass needle aligns itself with these lines of force.

■ How to use a compass

A compass needle always points north. Once you know which way north is you can figure out east, west and south.

■ A ship's compass

Long ago, sailing ships used magnetic compasses to help them find out where they were and how to get to where they wanted to go.

If you hold a compass when you are near the North Pole, the N needle of the compass will try to point straight to the ground.

7

What Kind of Material Are the Earth and Planets Made Of?

ANSWER Mercury, Venus, Earth and Mars are made mostly of rock. Jupiter, Saturn, Uranus and Neptune are made of different gases. Pluto, the most distant planet, is like an icy rock.

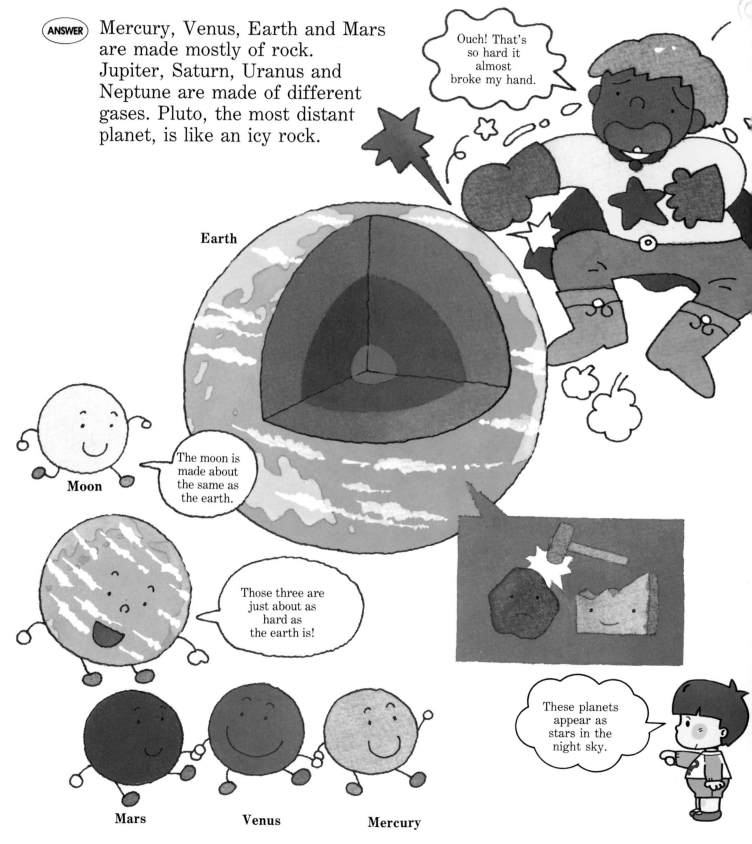

Ouch! That's so hard it almost broke my hand.

Earth

Moon

The moon is made about the same as the earth.

Those three are just about as hard as the earth is!

These planets appear as stars in the night sky.

Mars

Venus

Mercury

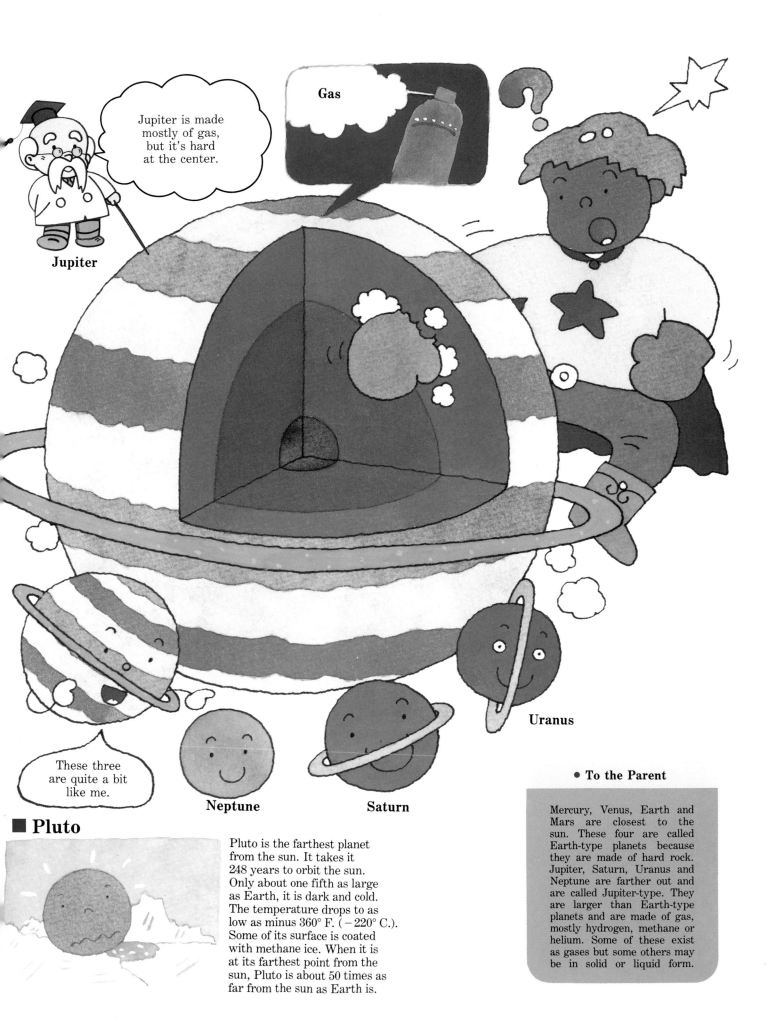

Jupiter is made mostly of gas, but it's hard at the center.

Gas

Jupiter

These three are quite a bit like me.

Uranus

Neptune   **Saturn**

■ Pluto

Pluto is the farthest planet from the sun. It takes it 248 years to orbit the sun. Only about one fifth as large as Earth, it is dark and cold. The temperature drops to as low as minus 360° F. (−220° C.). Some of its surface is coated with methane ice. When it is at its farthest point from the sun, Pluto is about 50 times as far from the sun as Earth is.

● **To the Parent**

Mercury, Venus, Earth and Mars are closest to the sun. These four are called Earth-type planets because they are made of hard rock. Jupiter, Saturn, Uranus and Neptune are farther out and are called Jupiter-type. They are larger than Earth-type planets and are made of gas, mostly hydrogen, methane or helium. Some of these exist as gases but some others may be in solid or liquid form.

How Is the Size Of the Earth Measured?

ANSWER The earth is too big to measure with a tape. Instead we must use mathematics. One way is to look at a star from two spots on the earth's surface. If we know the distance from one spot to the other we can figure out the earth's size.

A star is in the same place when viewed from any spot on the earth. Because of this we can use it to measure angles.

Look at a star from two places. Then find the angle between the zenith and the star for each location.

Find the angle between the zenith and a line to the star from spot A.

Zenith

Direction to a single star

Zenith

Now measure the angle between these two lines at location B.

If you could draw lines from point O to points A and B you would make the angle you need to figure out how big the earth is.

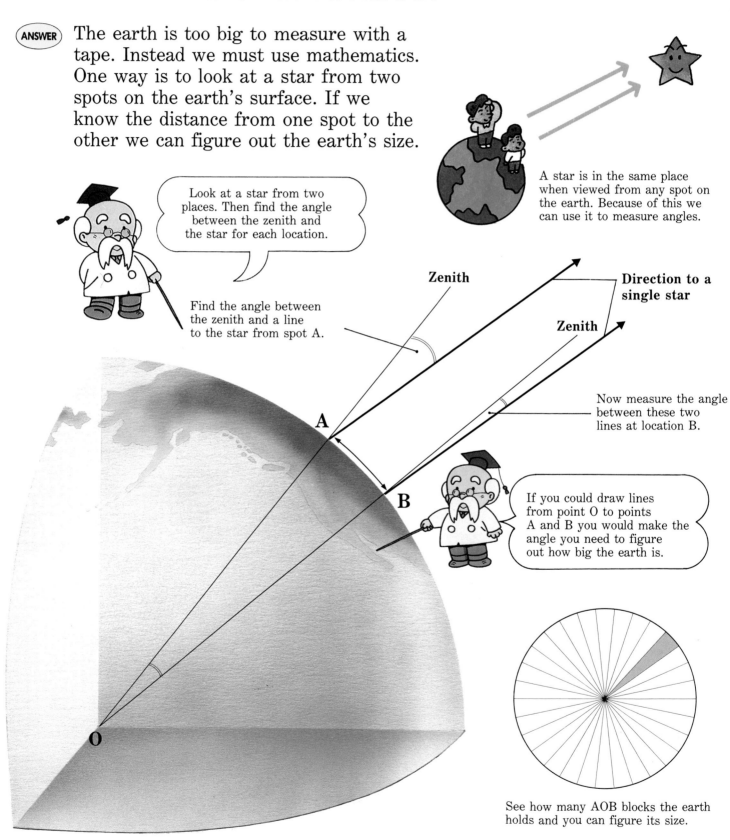

See how many AOB blocks the earth holds and you can figure its size.

■ Measuring the earth from a satellite

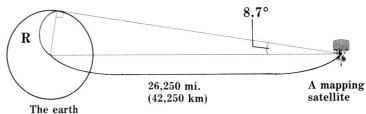

26,250 mi.
(42,250 km)

R

17.4°

Another way to measure the size of the earth is with the help of special satellites that are used for mapping. They observe the earth from 22,300 miles (35,900 km) in space. The satellite can measure the angles from opposite sides of the earth. Once scientists know this they can figure out the earth's radius. That's the distance from the earth's surface to its center. If you know the radius of a circle, you can use mathematics to figure out how far it measures around the outside. It takes three of these special satellites orbiting the earth to see the entire surface at one time.

8.7°

R

26,250 mi.
(42,250 km)

The earth

A mapping satellite

■ How an ancient Greek measured the earth

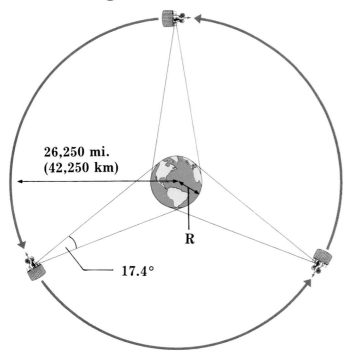

The Greek scholar Eratosthenes studied the shadow made by a tower in Alexandria, Egypt. He measured the angle that the shadow made on the first day of summer.

He knew that on the same day at the same time in Syene the sun was at its highest point. It shone straight down into a well, so it must be directly overhead.

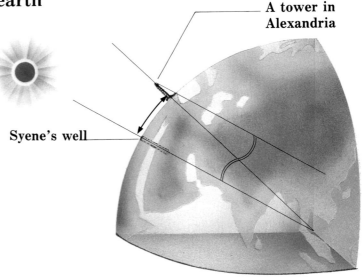

A tower in Alexandria

Syene's well

It was 500 miles (800 km) from Alexandria to Syene. The angle was a fiftieth of a circle. He multiplied 500 by 50 and found that the earth was 25,000 miles (40,000 km) around.

● To the Parent

We obviously cannot measure a thing as big as the earth with a tape measure, so we use mathematics to do it. But Eratosthenes' estimate, 2,200 years ago, was very near the 24,902 miles (40,075 km) now known to be the circumference of the earth at the equator. Today's equipment is so precise that we know that the earth at the equator is 26.7 miles (43 km) thicker than when it is measured from pole to pole.

How Were
The Oceans Made?

ANSWER The oceans were made when the earth was forming. For a long time the fiery hot earth was covered with thick clouds. As the earth cooled, rain fell from these clouds. The water flowed from higher places to lower ones, and as it got deeper it formed oceans. You can follow this process in the picture on this page.

As the earth spun it got smaller. The heavier materials went to the center and the lighter ones to the outside. This caused much pressure inside the earth. It started to heat up again, and water inside was forced out in volcanoes and through cracks in the earth's surface. The steam formed thick clouds and covered the earth.

The earth began as a hot cloud of swirling gas. In the cloud tiny bits of matter kept bumping into each other. As the cloud cooled, the matter began to stick together and form a bigger and bigger mass. All this time the mass was spinning, so the earth began to take on a round shape.

● **To the Parent**

When the earth was forming it was a great deal heavier and many, many times its present diameter. For millions of years it contracted, and the metallic elements sank inward while the lighter rocks and other materials were forced to the outside to form the crust. Pressures of this movement created temperatures so high that even rocks were molten. There was always a lot of water in the earth, but in those high temperatures it boiled away and became clouds. Rain that fell sizzled away to become clouds. It was millions of years before it became cool enough for rain to fall and remain on the earth.

As the earth became cool again these clouds also cooled and water began to fall to the surface as rain. This rain continued for a long, long time.

The water ran off to the low places and stayed there. When enough of it had come together this water became the oceans.

MINI-DATA

What if all the ice melted?

Some scientists believe the earth is warming up. If it ever became warm enough to melt all the ice at the North and South Poles, the ocean level would rise. Many coastal cities would be covered with water. Such a change would take thousands of years.

What Is the Ocean Floor Like?

ANSWER You might think that it's flat, but it's not. There's a mountain range under the ocean that's 40,000 miles (65,000 km) long. There's a big ditch, called a trench, that's six times larger than the Grand Canyon. There are even volcanoes on the ocean floor.

On the bottom of the ocean there are places from which lava spouts and where lava seeps back into the earth.

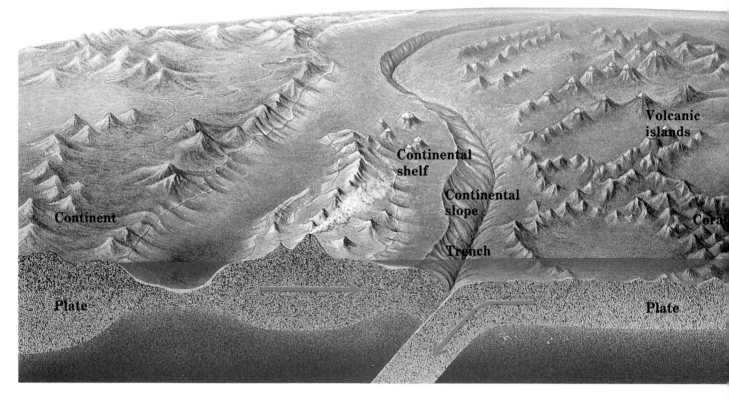

Continent

Continental shelf

Continental slope

Trench

Volcanic islands

Coral

Plate

Plate

▲ Coral reef

▲ Submerged coral reef

Trench

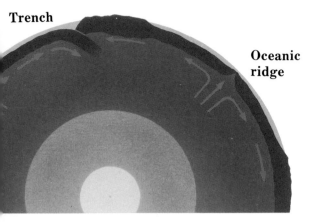

Oceanic ridge

Oceanic ridge

▲ **Submerged volcano**

 # How Deep Can We Go Into the Ocean?

Diving boats can go very deep if they are built to withstand enough pressure. Others are not as strong since they are not made for deep diving. The strongest may dive to 20,000 feet (6,000 m).

● **To the Parent**

Perhaps the most salient feature of the ocean bottom is a vast mountain chain. The main ridge, as it is called, runs from the Arctic Ocean down around the tip of Africa, then passes south of Australia and runs to a point west of the southern tip of South America. Then it turns north and finally runs up the west coast of the United States to the Alaska panhandle. Scientists believe that hot lava constantly pushes up through rifts in the ridges, spills over on each side and moves in both directions. It hardens on the lithospheric plates below the oceanic crust. These move across the sea floor at one half to three inches (1.3 to 7.6 cm) a year. When they meet, one dives under the other, creating a trench and triggering earthquakes. There are also more than a hundred volcanoes on the ocean floor, some so close to the surface that when they erupt they create islands. A volcano near Iceland on the Mid-Atlantic Ridge built such an island in 1963. The island, named Surtsey, is still above water.

❓ Did You Know That Oceans Flow?

ANSWER Though most water in the oceans appears to be standing still it is always moving in what we call currents. All oceans have currents, which are much like the currents that you see in rivers.

If you put a letter into a bottle and put it in the ocean, the current may take it to another land.

Ocean Currents

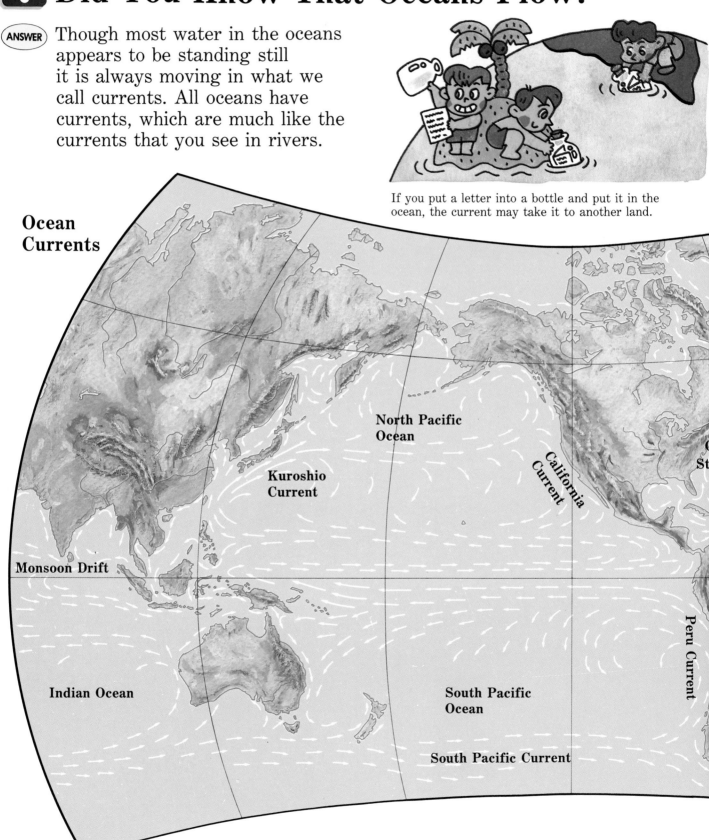

North Pacific Ocean

Kuroshio Current

California Current

G... Str...

Monsoon Drift

Indian Ocean

South Pacific Ocean

Peru Current

South Pacific Current

The arrows indicate ocean currents.

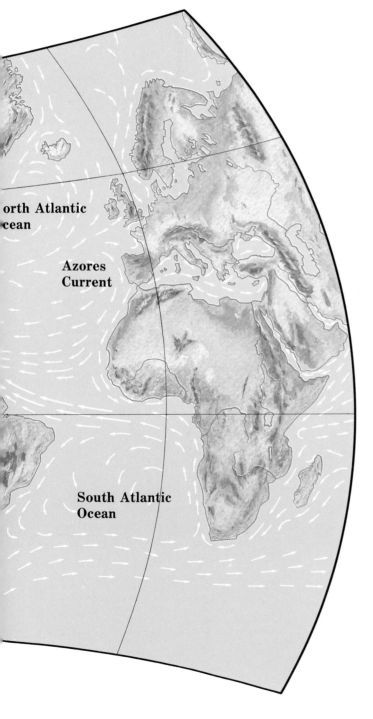

North Atlantic Ocean

Azores Current

South Atlantic Ocean

■ Why ocean currents occur

Strong, steady winds covering our planet can cause a current, but other forces make currents too.

The spinning of the earth keeps the waters in motion and is another cause of ocean currents.

■ The direction of currents

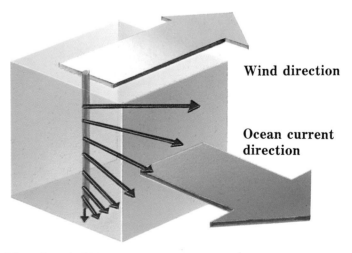

Wind direction

Ocean current direction

When the wind blows it pushes water closest to the surface along with it. But the spin of the earth causes it to flow in different directions.

? How Are Lakes Made?

ANSWER Lakes are formed in several ways. Some are made when water collects in craters of volcanoes or low, hollow places in the earth. Lakes can also be made by damming a river or sealing off a part of the ocean.

A caldera lake
This type of lake is created when water collects in the crater of a volcano.

A caldera lake

A dammed lake

An oxbow lake
This type of lake is made when part of a river has been dammed.

An oxbow lake

A lagoon

A lagoon
Sand has surrounded part of the sea to make this lake.

▲ A lagoon

● **To the Parent**

A lake usually refers to a body of water at least 15 feet (4.5 m) deep with plants growing on the bottom. If a body of water is less than this depth and has plant life it is a swamp. Since the United States has many rivers, many of its lakes are formed when these rivers are dammed. In other regions of the world, where volcanoes are more prevalent, lakes are created as water collects in volcanic craters.

18

A crater lake

The crater in the center of an inactive volcano has collected water. Crater Lake in Oregon was formed in such a manner.

A crater lake

A sag lake

America's deepest

The deepest lake in the United States is Oregon's Crater Lake. At 1,932 feet (589 m) it is almost twice as deep as the Eiffel Tower is high. Crater Lake is famous for its deep blue color.

A dammed lake

This river was dammed up by lava from a volcano that erupted many years ago.

▲ A crater lake

A sag lake

This is from a large hollow in the ground.

▲ A sag lake

▲ A dammed lake

19

How Are Rocks Formed?

(ANSWER) New rock is being made all the time. It begins as liquid rock, or magma, deep inside the earth. When it comes to the surface it cools and turns solid. Other forces such as erosion by wind and water also help make new rock. The photographs below show the three basic kinds of rock.

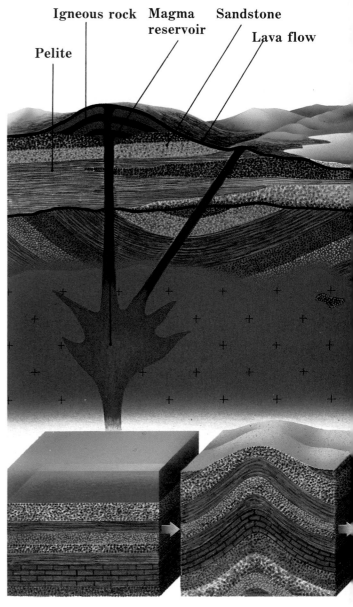

Pelite

Igneous rock   Magma reservoir   Sandstone   Lava flow

Earth and sand that collect in layers on the bottom of a lake or the ocean turn into sedimentary rock.

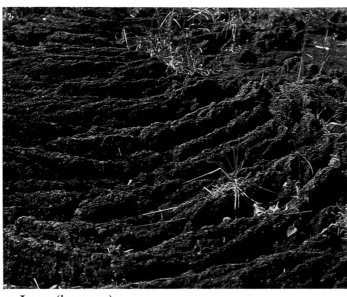

▲ Lava (igneous)

▲ Granite (igneous)

▲ Sandstone and pelite layer (sedimentary)

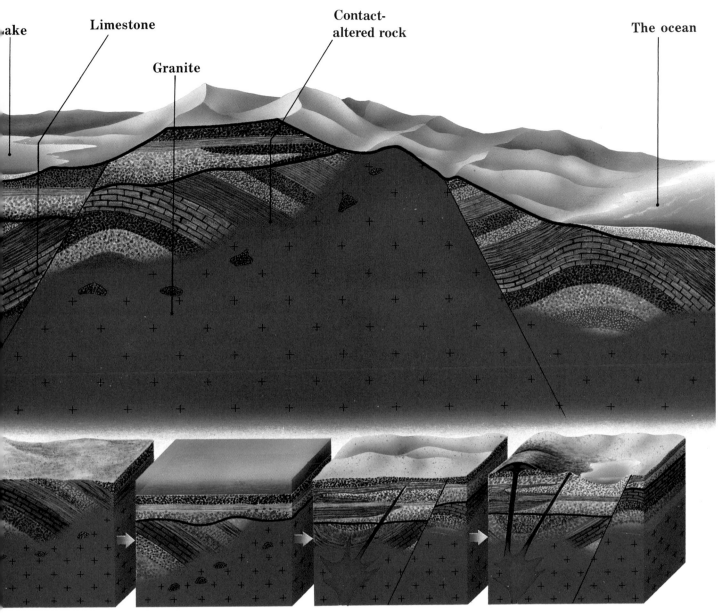

ake Limestone Granite Contact-altered rock The ocean

Pressure or the heat from magma can change sedimentary rock into metamorphic rock.

Liquid rock that cools underground or after erupting from a volcano becomes igneous rock.

▲ Metamorphic crystalline rock   ▲ Dike rock

● To the Parent

Rocks that form the surface of the earth are classified into igneous, sedimentary and metamorphic rock. If magma, which is formed deep inside the earth, surfaces and turns solid, it becomes igneous rock. If this is broken up by weathering or erosion, and these pieces are carried away by wind or water, they become sedimentary rock. If igneous or sedimentary rock is pushed underground by movements in the earth's crust, it is altered and becomes metamorphic. This change is caused by the pressure of the earth and the extremely high temperature of the molten magma inside of the earth.

21

❓ How Is Oil Made?

■ This is how oil is made

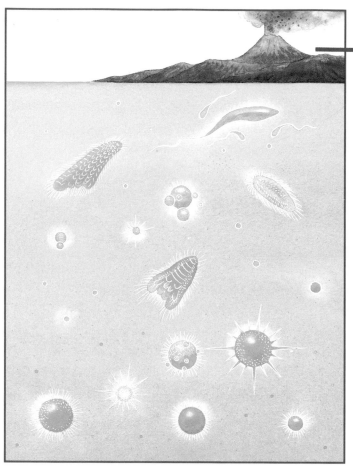

A very large number of things live in the water. Mostly they are different kinds of animals. These living things are the origin of oil. They can turn into oil in millions of years if conditions are right.

When these living organisms die they fall to the floor of the lake or ocean. As many years pass the number of these dead organisms increases. Eventually, as many, many more years pass they pile up in layers.

■ Places that produce a lot of oil

Oil is not found everywhere. In fact very few places produce oil. Most of these places are in the Middle East, such as Saudi Arabia and Iran. Over half of the oil produced in the world comes from this region. Places that do not have their own supply of oil must purchase their oil from other countries.

▼ Red marks show where oil is produced.

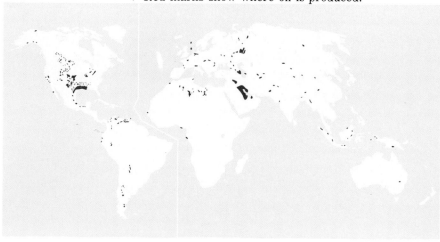

(ANSWER) When small plants, insects and animals die in the water they pile up on the bottom. Over a very long time these things are changed to oil by heat from the earth.

The layer of dead organisms gets even thicker when dirt piles up on top of it. The heat from the earth below it causes these things to rot and change into oil. This takes a very long time to happen.

Oil collects in certain places and seeps into the soil around it. When we find soil with a lot of oil in it, it often tells us that more oil may be buried below that. So we can then dig a hole and pump the oil out.

■ Where the oil is

While some countries have no oil supplies at all, others have a very large supply. The countries with the largest supplies of oil are Saudi Arabia, Kuwait, Iran, the U.S.S.R. and the United States. The Middle East alone produces more than half of the oil used throughout the world.

▲ **An offshore oil platform**

● **To the Parent**

Oil is primarily produced by dead plankton and algae, or seaweed. These accumulate on the bottom of the sea and are preserved as organic matter. They are the basic material for oil. As new layers of this organic matter are covered by the mud the pressure builds up. This organic matter decomposes and, due to heat and certain bacteria, it is changed into gas or oil. The oil then seeps into the soft soil and accumulates in certain places. The countries that produce most of the oil are located in the Middle East and account for more than 50% of the world's oil output.

❓ How Is Coal Formed?

■ This is how coal is made

There was a time long, long ago when there were many trees growing in some places on the earth.

As those trees died they fell, and after a while they became buried under the ground.

■ Trees that became coal

The coal we dig up now comes from trees that grew in thick forests more than 300 million years ago. In time all of them died. During the many changes in the earth's crust over the years they were buried and turned into coal.

▶ The trees that turned into coal looked like this.

▲ **Tree bark fossil**

Trees that grew long, long ago were buried deep under the ground. The earth's heat changed them into coal. This process took place very slowly for many years.

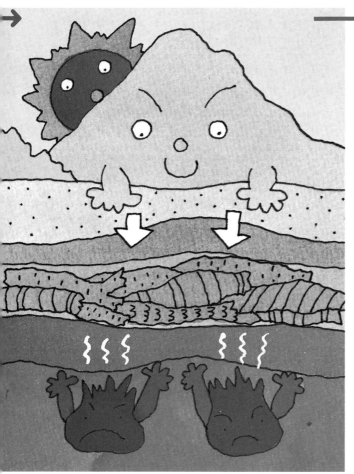

As many, many years passed, the heat of the earth changed those buried trees into coal.

Coal is usually buried under the ground, so we have to dig it out and bring it up to the surface.

MINI-DATA
An easy way to dig coal

There are some countries where coal can be dug up without making a deep shaft into the earth. The coal is dug right off the earth's surface. This method is known as open-pit mining.

●To the Parent

Coal is created from dead trees that have been buried. When trees fell into water in marshlands they decomposed and were absorbed into a mixture called marl. That is a combination of clay, limestone and sand. This conversion took place due to the action of certain micro-organisms, such as bacteria. Over a great span of time other matter accumulated on top of the marl, burying it deeper. As heat from inside the earth raised the temperature, water, hydrogen and nitrogen were removed from the marl, leaving it rich in carbon. This is what we call coal. Most of the world's coal comes from trees that were growing more than 300 million years ago.

❓ How Are Limestone Caves Made?

■ How rain creates caves

When rain gets into hollows or cracks in a formation of limestone the rock starts to dissolve little by little. The hollows and cracks become bigger and bigger. In this manner large holes are made under the ground. They eventually become limestone caves.

ANSWER Limestone dissolves very easily. Water erosion can wear it away. When rainwater soaks into a formation of limestone, bits of rock dissolve. If the holes get big enough they become caves.

● **To the Parent**

Rainwater and groundwater contain carbon dioxide, which is a weak acid. Limestone is dissolved by this acidic water. The water flows into cracks in limestone and dissolves it little by little. Caves, like many other of nature's processes, take ages to complete.

▲ Limestone deposits that look like daggers and hang down from the top of a cave are called stalactites. The ones that stick up from the floor are called stalagmites.

Caves may have strange features. Erosion sculpts designs on their walls. Caves with water often have fish that are blind from living in total darkness.

27

How Does a Geyser Shoot Water So High Into the Air?

ANSWER A geyser is a hot spring that spouts hot water as high as 1,000 feet (300 m) into the sky. It forms when hot water and gases collect in a deep hollow in the ground. When enough steam and air pressure build up in the hole, the water shoots up into the air.

Some geysers erupt on a dependable schedule.

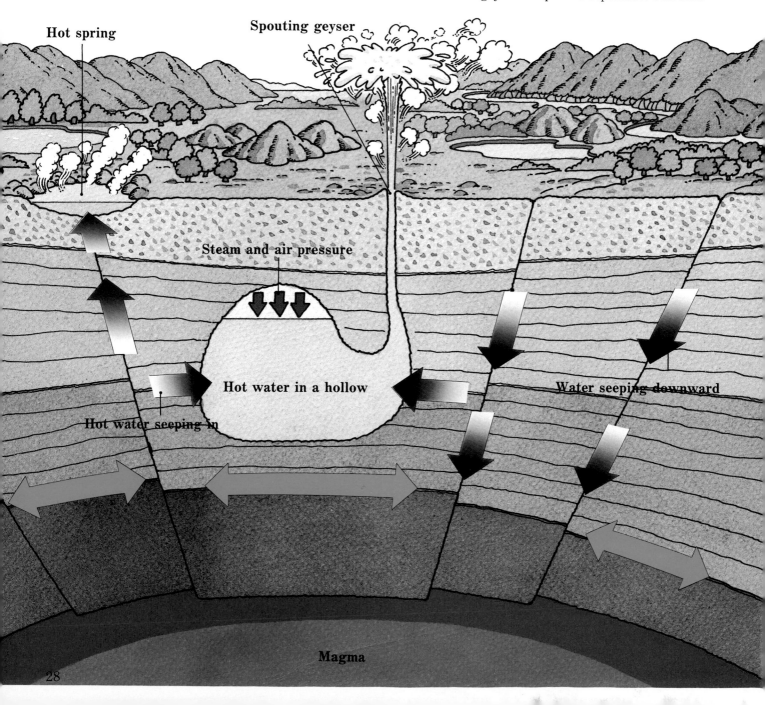

Hot spring

Spouting geyser

Steam and air pressure

Hot water in a hollow

Hot water seeping in

Water seeping downward

Magma

How a Geyser Spews Water

When a geyser spouts water, there's always a little water left in the hollow. The hot magma heats the water in the hollow. More water seeps into the hollow and traps the steam and air. When the pressure of the steam becomes strong enough, it forces the water out of the spout. This is the geyser you see shooting up into the air, and it is repeated again and again.

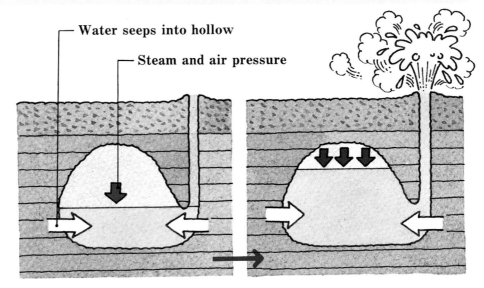

Water seeps into hollow

Steam and air pressure

Old Faithful, a big tourist attraction

▲ Yellowstone's famous geyser erupts every 33 to 93 minutes.

There are 200 geysers and hundreds of smaller thermal springs in Yellowstone National Park, most of which is in the northwest corner of Wyoming. The park attracts crowds of tourists.

● **To the Parent**

Geysers spout in different cycles. Some spout every few minutes. Others may spout at much less frequent intervals. They also shoot water to different heights. Some spout water only a few inches. But others may shoot water as high as two to three hundred feet (60 to 90 m). A geyser in New Zealand spewed water as high as 1,000 feet (300 m) for a few years before it tapered off.

How High Does the Atmosphere Go?

(ANSWER) The earth is surrounded by the air we breathe. This mixture of air and water vapor is what we call the atmosphere. It is thickest near the surface of the earth but gets thinner the higher we go. There is very little air at all above 600 miles (1,000 km).

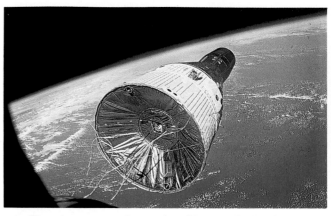

▲ The air seems to be a misty blue on the horizon.

■ The layers of the atmosphere

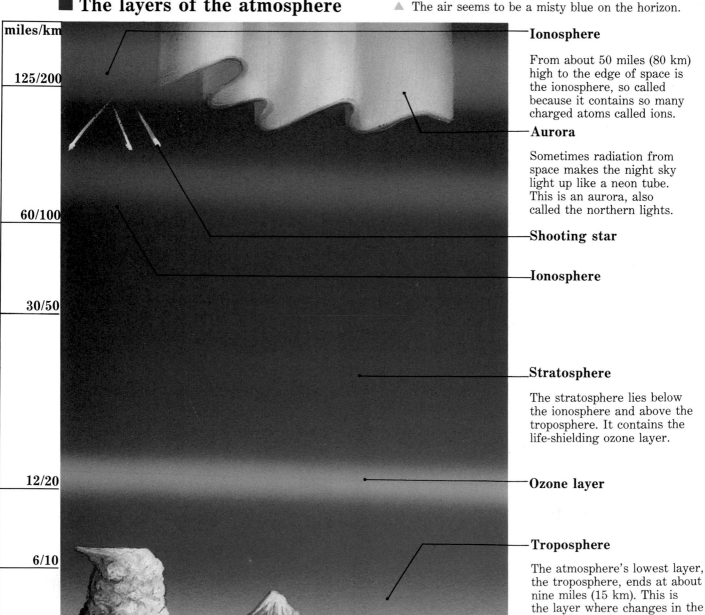

Ionosphere

From about 50 miles (80 km) high to the edge of space is the ionosphere, so called because it contains so many charged atoms called ions.

Aurora

Sometimes radiation from space makes the night sky light up like a neon tube. This is an aurora, also called the northern lights.

Shooting star

Ionosphere

Stratosphere

The stratosphere lies below the ionosphere and above the troposphere. It contains the life-shielding ozone layer.

Ozone layer

Troposphere

The atmosphere's lowest layer, the troposphere, ends at about nine miles (15 km). This is the layer where changes in the earth's weather are determined.

miles/km

125/200

60/100

30/50

12/20

6/10

■ Atmospheric gases closest to earth

Nitrogen 78.09%

Oxygen 20.94%

- Argon 0.93%
- Carbon dioxide 0.03%
- Neon 0.0018%
- Helium 0.0005%
- Hydrogen 0.00005%
- Other gases

The atmosphere close to the earth is made up mostly of nitrogen and oxygen. It contains a number of other gases, but they are present in much smaller amounts.

■ A shooting star glows as it burns

Meteors from space usually burn up in the mesosphere, where the air becomes dense enough to create lots of friction. This is the lowest part of the ionosphere.

Do You Know How Much the Atmosphere Weighs?

At sea level, where air is heaviest, a cubic foot (.03m³) of air weighs about an ounce and a fourth (35 g). The air exerts a pressure of almost 15 pounds per square inch (103 kPa). Our body responds by exerting an equal outward pressure of its own to balance the pressure the atmosphere puts on it.

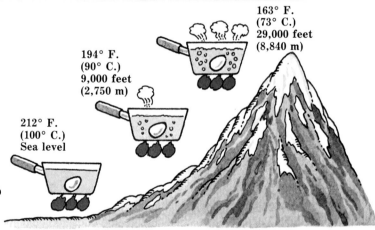

163° F. (73° C.) 29,000 feet (8,840 m)

194° F. (90° C.) 9,000 feet (2,750 m)

212° F. (100° C.) Sea level

Water boils at 212° F. (100° C.) at sea level, but if it is boiled at higher elevations the boiling temperature decreases.

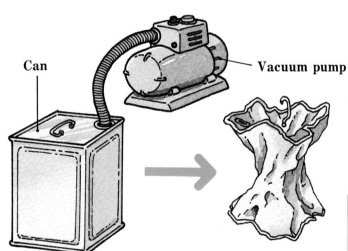

Can

Vacuum pump

If you pump all the air out of a can, the can will be crushed by pressure exerted on it by the air outside while there is no pressure inside the can to offset it.

? Why Does a Low-Pressure Area Usually Bring Rain?

ANSWER A low-pressure area is one where the atmospheric, or air, pressure is lower than areas around it. When this occurs, air flows into the low-pressure zone. This causes air currents to rise. Vapor in these currents cools and forms clouds that produce rain.

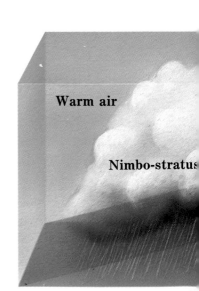

Rising air

Low Pressure

Air from surrounding areas is drawn to the center of a low-pressure area.

Cold air flow

Cold front moving

■ How cold and warm fronts differ

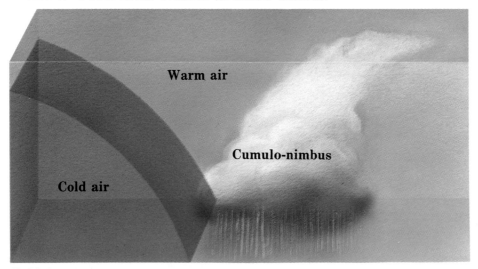

Warm air

Cold air

Cumulo-nimbus

Warm air

Nimbo-stratus

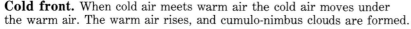

Cold front. When cold air meets warm air the cold air moves under the warm air. The warm air rises, and cumulo-nimbus clouds are formed.

■ A nontropical cyclone

A cyclone occurs when warm air and cool air meet. Outside the tropics this is called a nontropical cyclone. Normally it is not very strong. A warm or cold front usually accompanies a nontropical cyclone.

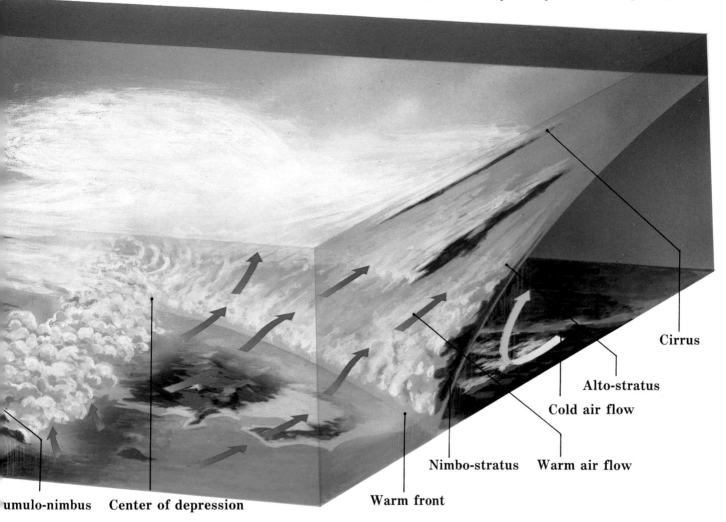

Cirrus

Alto-stratus

Cold air flow

Nimbo-stratus Warm air flow

umulo-nimbus   Center of depression

Warm front

Cold air

Warm front. When warm air meets cool air the warm air moves over the cool air. This causes stratified clouds to form near the warm front.

● To the Parent

A low-pressure area is an area in which air pressure is lower than in the atmosphere surrounding it. Like water flowing downhill, the outside air flows toward the center of the depression, rising and cooling as it does. The vapor in the air becomes water or ice, and rain-producing clouds result. A depression that forms in the Temperate Zone is often accompanied by warm or cold fronts. Clouds form along these fronts. In the Northern Hemisphere the air in a low-pressure area will flow in a counterclockwise direction. In the Southern Hemisphere, however, the air moves in a clockwise direction.

? How Does a Tornado Start?

(ANSWER) Usually cold air will flow under warm air. When cold air goes over hot air, conditions are right for a tornado. It will occur if hot air rushes upward at great speed. More air then rushes in from the sides creating a huge, spinning funnel of wind. A tornado's winds can turn at 250 miles per hour (400 km/h). The storms can strike anywhere but they are most common in the Midwestern states.

▲ A twister roars across the United States.

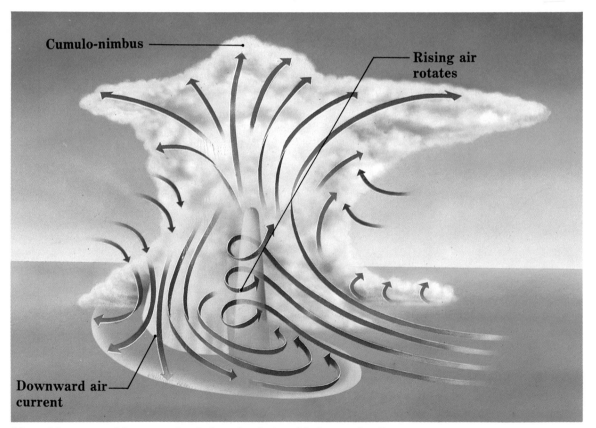

Cumulo-nimbus

Rising air rotates

Downward air current

Air rushing upward in a cumulo-nimbus cloud gives birth to a deadly storm.

● To the Parent

Tornadoes are the most powerful storms on earth. The air pressure inside the funnel is so low that houses in a tornado's path have been known to explode from the pressure of expanding air inside the house. The winds are so powerful that they have driven straws into tree trunks. The storm carries assorted heavy things with it, dropping them here and there as it goes, often with damage to property or injury to people or animals that might otherwise have gone unscathed.

The funnel may range from 50 to 1,200 feet (15 to 365 m) wide.

A tornado zips across the land at speeds up to 70 mph (110 km/h).

It may last only a few minutes, but those can be catastrophic.

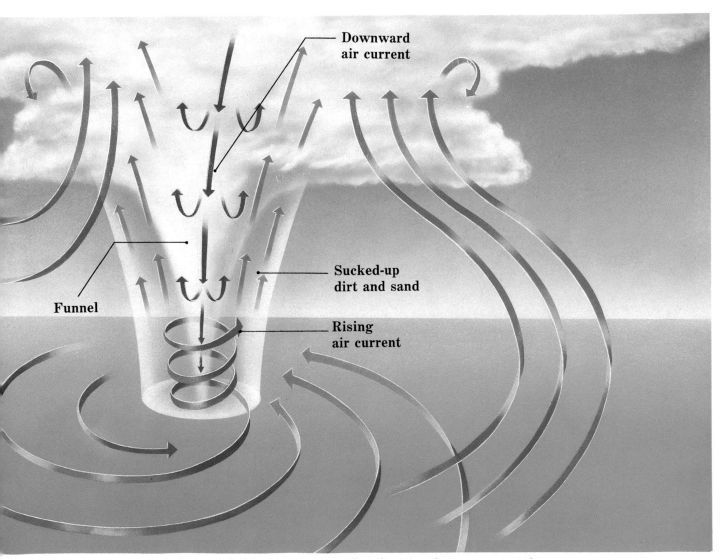

The storm sucks up everything in its path. Most air moves up, but there is a down current at the center.

❓ What Causes A Glacier?

ANSWER In the far north and high in the mountains snow doesn't melt in the summer. Instead it freezes and forms huge fields of ice. From high places these ice fields slide downward. These rivers of ice are glaciers. They are so big and hard that they can change the land. Many of the strange rock formations around the world were carved by glaciers.

I wish I had brought my sled!

U-shaped valley

U-shaped valleys are carved by glaciers moving downward.

▲ This glacier is on Mt. Rosa, Switzerland, near Mont Blanc.

● **To the Parent**

Glaciers, which cover 10% of the earth's land surface, form in high mountains or in areas far from the equator where the snow never melts. The snow line is the minimum elevation at which snow will not melt. If there is heavy snowfall above this line annually a glacier will develop. The bottom layers of snow are compressed as snow accumulates, and two big layers of ice form. When it is massive enough the glacier slowly descends. It may travel from a few dozen to as many as hundreds of yards yearly.

Cirque

Glacier

Moraine

A cirque is a hollow that has been carved out by a glacier.

Patterns and folds on a glacier's surface are made by crushed rock.

Moraines are made of rock and other debris washed down by glaciers.

■ Glaciers and the snow line

Above a certain altitude snow never melts. This is called the snow line. Glaciers form above this line and melt below it.

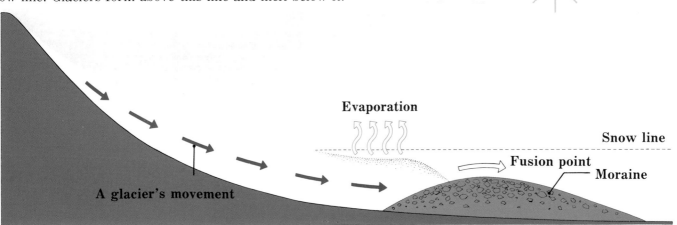

Evaporation

Snow line

Fusion point

Moraine

A glacier's movement

Why Do We See a Mirage When Nothing Is There?

(ANSWER) Sometimes when we're outside, we see a pool of water or an island that actually is not there. We call this a mirage. A mirage is nothing but an optical illusion. When light passes through layers of hot and cold air it bends. This fools our eyes and we see something that doesn't exist.

■ The desert's a mirage maker

People in a desert might think that they can see trees or bodies of water far away.

As they walk toward the trees or water the vision vanishes. A mirage is never really there.

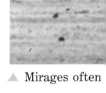

▲ Mirages often

Here's how layers of air create a mirage

When sea water is very cold the air above it is also cold. When the air above that is warm two layers of air form, one hot and one cold. If light reflects off a faraway object, such as an island, it will bend as it passes through the layers of air. Then the island will appear to be somewhere it is not. It could even seem to be floating in the sky.

occur on African plains. Their shimmer makes them look like pools of water. This type of mirage is called a false surface.

Let's find out about false surfaces

When the ground is hot the air just above it is warm. But resting on top of the warm air is a layer of cooler air, and the layers touch each other. Reflected light passing through these two layers is bent, and we think that we see a surface where one doesn't really exist.

▲ **A false surface.** That's not water on the road.

39

? How and When Did the Universe Start?

ANSWER Most scientists believe that the universe began about 20 billion years ago. At first it was very, very small, and it was made of completely different materials than it is today. Soon after it began, it started to spread out very rapidly. This growth is now called the Big Bang, because it was so fast it was like an explosion.

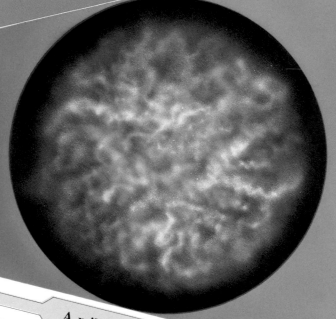

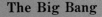
The beginning

A million years later

Several million y

The Big Bang

Before the Big Bang, the universe was a much smaller ball. Then it exploded, and there was an incredibly hot mass of light. Scientists believe that it was billions and billions of degrees Fahrenheit. There is nothing in the universe today that is nearly as hot as that.

The universe then began to clear up

After the Big Bang, the universe continued to spread out and to slowly cool. At first the universe seemed like a hazy mass. As time passed, parts of it became clearer.

A supergalactic group

The early universe had no clear shape or structure. Scientists describe this as being in a state of chaos. As the universe kept spreading out, a cloudlike mass of gases began to form. This bunch of gases became what is called a supergalactic group. Although the universe was taking shape, it was a long way from being like anything we know.

• To the Parent

The universe began about 20 billion years ago as a very small, very hot ball of fire. The Big Bang theory describes the explosive expansion of this ball. It is not known how the ball of fire came into existence or why the Big Bang took place. Many scientists believe that the universe is expanding at a very high speed and that it will never stop expanding.

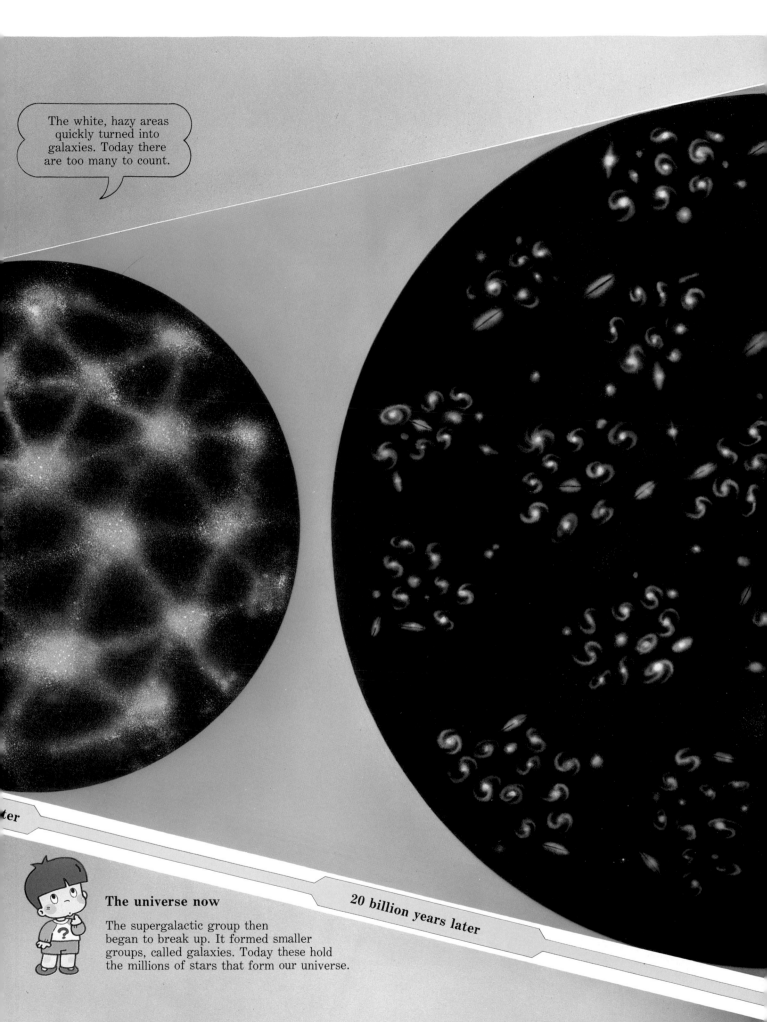

The white, hazy areas quickly turned into galaxies. Today there are too many to count.

ter

The universe now

The supergalactic group then began to break up. It formed smaller groups, called galaxies. Today these hold the millions of stars that form our universe.

20 billion years later

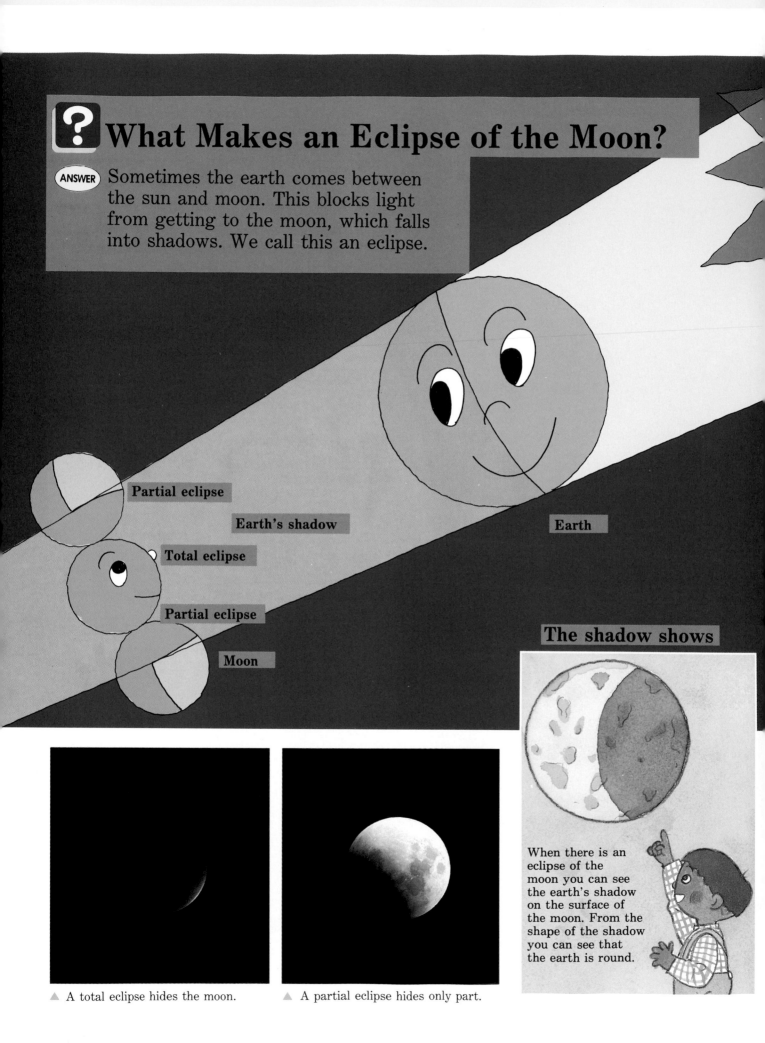

❓ What Makes an Eclipse of the Moon?

ANSWER Sometimes the earth comes between the sun and moon. This blocks light from getting to the moon, which falls into shadows. We call this an eclipse.

Partial eclipse

Earth's shadow

Total eclipse

Partial eclipse

Moon

Earth

The shadow shows

When there is an eclipse of the moon you can see the earth's shadow on the surface of the moon. From the shape of the shadow you can see that the earth is round.

▲ A total eclipse hides the moon.

▲ A partial eclipse hides only part.

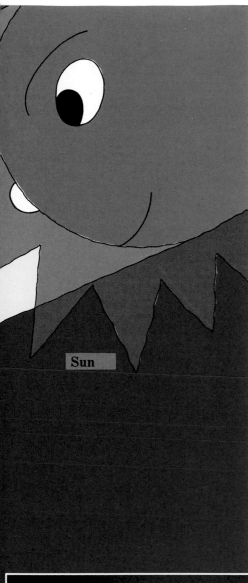

■ Your own eclipse

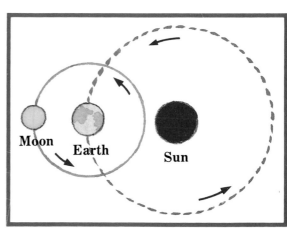

A house that blocks sunlight casts a shadow on the street. A child walking into the shadow is in darkness just like the moon during an eclipse.

■ Why eclipses occur

When the sun, earth and moon are in one line the moon is covered by the earth's shadow, and that is called an eclipse of the moon.

Moon   Earth   Sun

◄ **Progress of an eclipse of the moon**

During a total eclipse the moon is completely dark. But it looks red, not black. This is because light from the sun is diffused or scattered when it enters the earth's atmosphere so that just red light rays get into the shadow. So the moon looks red.

● **To the Parent**

An eclipse of the moon occurs when the sun, earth and moon are in alignment. The earth blocks sunlight from reaching the moon, so the moon falls into the shadow of the earth. When the moon is entirely in deep shadow it is called a total eclipse. A partial eclipse of the moon is when only a part of the moon is in deep shadow. In an eclipse the moon looks darker than usual.

How Far Away Are the Stars?

ANSWER That depends on the star. The sun is our nearest star. Its light reaches us in eight minutes. Other stars are so far away that their light takes years to reach us.

Sirius
8.7
light years

Altair
16 light years

Vega
25 light years

Alpha in Centaurus
4.3 light years

Pluto
5 hours
27 minutes

The sun
8 minutes
19 seconds

The moon
1.3
seconds

Figures are based on the speed of light, 186,000 miles (300,000 km) per second.

How to measure a star's distance

When we know one distance we can often use it to figure out another. Suppose two people stand along a road and face a tree. We know how far apart the people are. We measure the angle formed by the tree and points A and B. We can then calculate the distance to the tree. We measure distance to stars the same way. We know the distance from the earth to the sun. We measure the angle of the star to earth on opposite sides of the earth's orbit around the sun. We then use mathematics to figure out the distance to the stars.

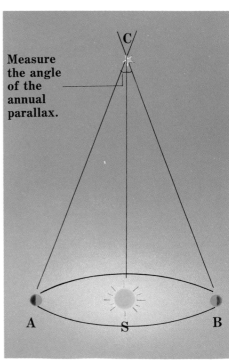

Measure the angle of the annual parallax.

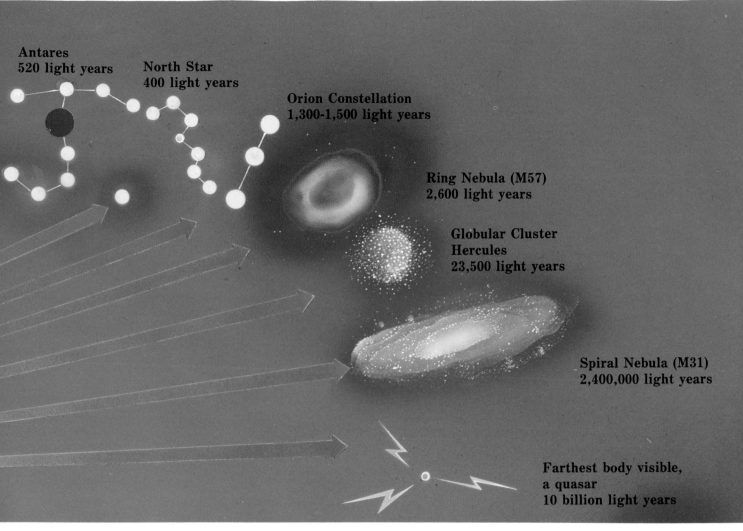

Antares
520 light years

North Star
400 light years

Orion Constellation
1,300-1,500 light years

Ring Nebula (M57)
2,600 light years

Globular Cluster
Hercules
23,500 light years

Spiral Nebula (M31)
2,400,000 light years

Farthest body visible,
a quasar
10 billion light years

■ Another way to measure distance

Scientists sometimes use a
star's light to figure out its
distance from earth. They
study the light from a faraway
star. They can measure how
bright a star was when it
formed. If they compare that
to its brightness today, they
can calculate how far away it is.

A light year is the distance light
travels in one year at about
186,000 miles (300,000 km) per second.

● **To the Parent**

The distance of stars from the earth
is too far to be measured directly.
The distance of nearby stars can be
figured using the annual parallax,
but the angle is not nearly large
enough to calculate the distance of
faraway stars in this way. Distances
of faraway stars are calculated by
looking at the light spectrum of a
star to find its stellar magnitude.

❓ Why Do People Float Inside a Spaceship?

ANSWER When a spaceship is in orbit everything inside it is weightless, even the astronauts. Because of the pull of gravity the spaceship and the people inside are "falling" around the earth. When things are falling like this they're weightless and can float.

As long as the apple and the scale are falling, the apple's weight is zero.

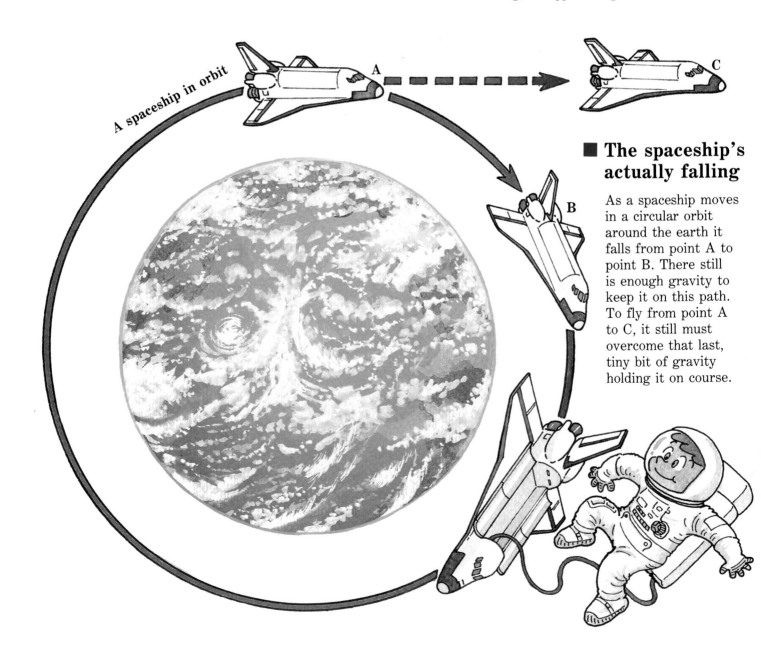

A spaceship in orbit

A

C

B

■ The spaceship's actually falling

As a spaceship moves in a circular orbit around the earth it falls from point A to point B. There still is enough gravity to keep it on this path. To fly from point A to C, it still must overcome that last, tiny bit of gravity holding it on course.

Strange Things Happen When You're Weightless

On earth objects fall because of the pull of gravity. But in space, with no gravity, you'll find that things happen differently.

Anything that isn't tied down will float. If you let go of a tool or anything else it floats without falling.

▲ An astronaut works out inside a spaceship in orbit.

A weightless spider spins a web

An American high school student named Judith Miles suggested an experiment to be done in the space shuttle. She wanted to know whether a spider could spin a web in the weightless conditions of space. The first time the spider tried, it couldn't spin a web. The second time it tried, it was successful.

If you spill water it separates into drops of different sizes, and they float around in front of you.

▲ **Spinning a weightless web**

• To the Parent

A spacecraft in orbit around the earth is in a free fall along a curved path that corresponds to the earth's curvature. As in a free-falling elevator, the effect of gravity is neutralized in the orbiting spacecraft, and a state of weightlessness is produced. Because the people and objects inside the spacecraft are not resisting the pull of gravity, the feeling of weight as experienced on earth is no longer present. Instead they seem weightless.

How Many Colors Does Sunlight Have?

ANSWER The light that comes from the sun is a mixture of red, orange, yellow, green, blue, indigo and violet light. They're the same colors you see in a rainbow. With a prism you can see those seven colors separately. When sunlight goes through a prism it bends so that each color comes out at a different angle. Violet light bends the most and red bends the least.

Separating light this way into seven colors is called dispersion.

▲ The seven colors separate when they go through a prism.

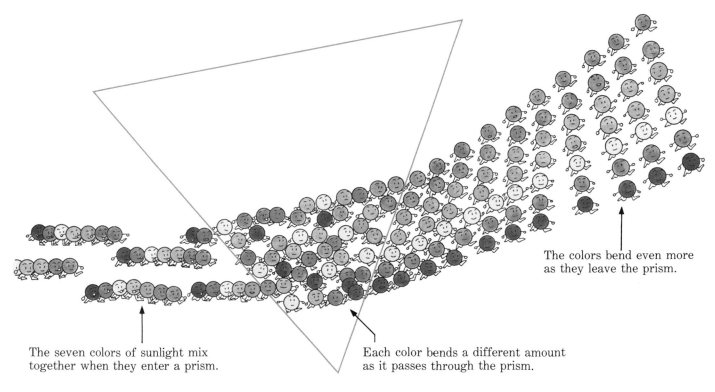

The colors bend even more as they leave the prism.

The seven colors of sunlight mix together when they enter a prism.

Each color bends a different amount as it passes through the prism.

48

Sometimes you can see a rainbow in the sky after it stops raining. The rainbow is formed as sunlight passes through raindrops. Like thousands of tiny prisms the raindrops make the light separate into seven colors. One side of the rainbow's band of colors is violet and the other is red, with all the other colors arranged in between. Did you know that you can create the rainbow's colors yourself? Here are three ways.

Tilt a mirror in a bowl of water so that it reflects sunlight on a wall. You'll see seven separate colors.

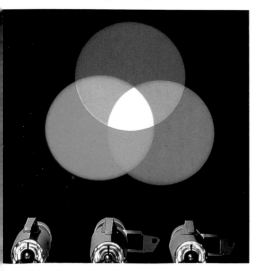

Stand with your back to the sun and sprinkle water. You can see a rainbow in the falling drops of water.

If sunlight passes through a small hole onto a round flask of water, you'll see the seven colors reflected.

Why Don't We Usually See Sunlight as Seven Colors?

Red, blue and green are called the primary colors of light. They are the colors from which all other colors are made. When the three primary colors are mixed, white is produced.

▲ White is produced where the red, blue and green overlap.

A top colored red, blue and green.

When the top spins, it seems to be colored white.

Let's mix the three primary colors of light so that we end up with white.

● **To the Parent**

Sunlight appears to be white but is actually a mixture of seven colors. We can prove this by using a prism to disperse light into its seven component colors. Dispersion occurs because each color is refracted, or bent, by a different amount as it passes through the prism, because each color has a wavelength that is different from all the others. Sunlight can also be dispersed when it is passed through water.

Why Is Some Smoke Black But Other Smoke Is Gray or White?

ANSWER The color depends on what's in the smoke. When smoke is white it contains moisture. When it's black the smoke is carrying soot. And when it's gray the smoke has ashes in it.

▲ Factory chimneys make a lot of smoke.

Smoke, which has water
vapor in it, may look
blue. Sunlight, you will
remember, is made up of
seven colors. The blue
is scattered when sunlight
hits the vapor in the
smoke. But you see this
only when the sky is dark,
the way it is at dusk. At
some other time of day
the smoke would look white.

Smoke is black if it doesn't have enough oxygen

Oxygen is necessary for anything to burn. When a
fire gets enough oxygen everything burns up.
That's called perfect combustion. But if there's
not enough oxygen, not everything burns. Some of it
is turned into soot, which makes the smoke black.

If the fire doesn't
get enough oxygen
the smoke will have
lots of soot in it.

• To the Parent

The color of smoke depends on the
composition of the smoke. White
smoke contains moisture from damp
fuel or hydrogen released as the fuel
burns. Black smoke contains carbon
particles produced by imperfect
combustion. Gray smoke contains ash
from poor-quality fuel. Sometimes
white smoke looks blue because the
blue component of sunlight is
dispersed by the moisture in the
smoke. Seen from a different angle,
however, the smoke will look white.

❓ Why Can't We See a Smell?

ANSWER Something smells when bits of it, called molecules, float in the air. Molecules are much too small to see. When they enter your nose, nerves send a message to your brain. When that happens, you smell something.

▲ Flowers have a very nice smell.

What's the Difference Between a Pleasant Smell And an Unpleasant One?

A pleasant smell makes us feel good, but a bad smell bothers us. Although we may not like bad smells, sometimes they help us. For instance a bad smell can warn us that food is spoiled.

We usually think that flowers smell nice and spoiled food smells bad.

A smell that's pleasant to one person may not be so pleasant to someone else. Food that we like smells good to us, but food that we don't like doesn't smell good.

Whether certain things smell good or bad depends on our own tastes.

Musk is one of the things perfume is made of. It comes from a musk deer. Straight from the deer, musk has a strong, unpleasant smell. But if the musk is thinned with alcohol the smell becomes a nice one. Too many molecules can make a bad smell even if it's something that usually smells good to us.

Natural musk is too strong.   Diluted musk smells good.

The musk deer lives in Asia. We get musk only from the male deer.

● **To the Parent**

Smell is the detection of chemicals in the air by sensitive nerves behind the nose. Molecules that are too small to see are released by food, flowers and other aromatic sources. They float through the air until they reach the olfactory cells in the nasal cavity. At that point the molecules stimulate certain nerves, which in turn send signals to the brain, resulting in the perception of smell.

53

❓ Why Does a Golf Ball Have Dimples?

ANSWER The small hollows on the surface of a golf ball are called dimples. They make the golf ball travel farther through the air. A ball with dimples travels three times as far as one that doesn't have them.

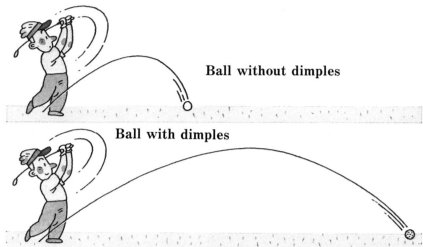

Ball without dimples

Ball with dimples

Inside a golf ball

In the center of a golf ball is a hard rubber core that's wrapped with layers of thin rubber string. On top of that is the surface layer, or cover, which has dimples in it. How deep the dimples are and how they're arranged on the surface is different with different kinds of golf balls. But those are important questions for golfers, because they determine how high and how far a golf ball will go.

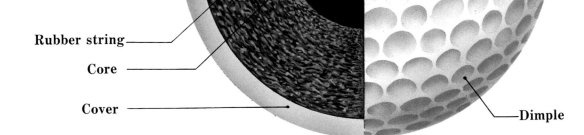

Rubber string

Core

Cover

Dimple

Why Does a Ball With Dimples Go Farther?

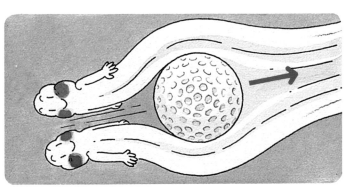

A ball forces air out of the way. The dimples help the air move quickly behind the ball so it travels faster.

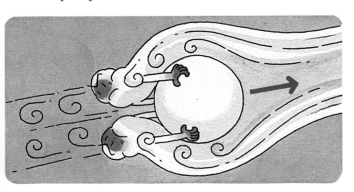

If there are no dimples the air can't get back behind the ball as quickly, so the ball doesn't move as fast.

As a ball flies through the air it rotates in reverse. This is called back spin. Back spin is the motion that helps lift the ball.

Dynamic lift is what makes kites and airplanes fly too.

● To the Parent

An old ball that has scars on its surface will go farther through the air than a smooth new ball. When golf players discovered this they began cutting notches on the surface of their golf balls, and manufacturers soon began putting dimples on the balls' surface. The depth and arrangement of the dimples are based on the laws of aerodynamics. A difference of only 1/1000 of an inch in the depth or the arrangement of the dimples affects the ball's trajectory.

Why Does a Tennis Ball Curve If It Is Hit With a Slicing Motion?

(ANSWER) When you hit a tennis ball with a slicing stroke it starts to spin. The spinning ball curves through the air. If you're right-handed the ball curves to the left. But if you're left-handed it curves to the right.

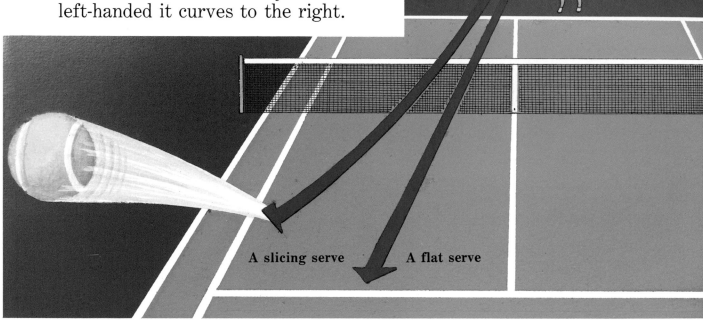

A slicing serve   A flat serve

■ How to make a slicing serve

The racket swings downward and strikes the ball so that it spins to the right.

The ball spins to the right when it's struck.

■ Here's why the ball curves

A spinning ball causes the air to flow faster on one side. It's pulled toward the faster air and it curves.

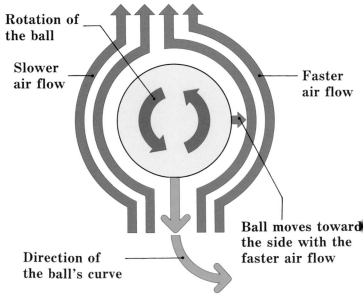

Rotation of the ball

Slower air flow

Faster air flow

Ball moves toward the side with the faster air flow

Direction of the ball's curve

Why Does Serving the Ball With Top-spin Make It Fall So Fast?

The top-spin makes the air move slower above the ball and faster below. The ball is pulled toward the faster air and drops quickly.

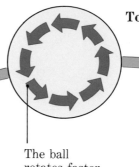

Top-spin serve

The ball rotates faster.

A flat serve makes the ball rotate normally. There's no downward pull on it, so the ball doesn't fall very fast.

Flat serve

The ball rotates more slowly with a flat serve.

■ How to hit a top-spin serve

The face of the racket should hit the ball from bottom left to top right.

That makes the ball jump upward when it's hit.

■ Why does the ball fall so fast?

The ball moves toward the side with the faster air flow, so it's pulled downward and falls quickly.

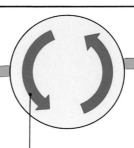

Direction of rotation

Slower flow of air

Faster flow of air

Direction of pull on ball

• To the Parent

A slice by a right-handed person, from his perspective, makes a tennis ball rotate to the right. This rotation increases the speed of the air flowing around the left side of the ball. This faster air flow in turn decreases the air pressure and pulls the ball in that direction.

How Do Fishing Boats Find Fish When the Ocean Is So Big?

(ANSWER) They use a fishfinder. It's a device that sends out sound waves. The waves bounce off schools of fish and are reflected back to the boat. The reflections are like echoes, but they appear on the fishfinder's screen and show people where the fish are.

▲ It's sort of like a TV screen.

The fishfinder uses colors to show where the fish are. Red shows where many fish are, yellow shows where few are, and blue shows places without any fish.

▲ Fish show up on the screen.

ANSWER 2 They use satellite information. Fish swim in parts of the ocean where the temperature is best for them. Some satellites can read the ocean temperatures. With that information people know where schools of fish are likely to be.

A satellite can measure the water's temperature.

Information collected by the satellite is sent to a ground station.

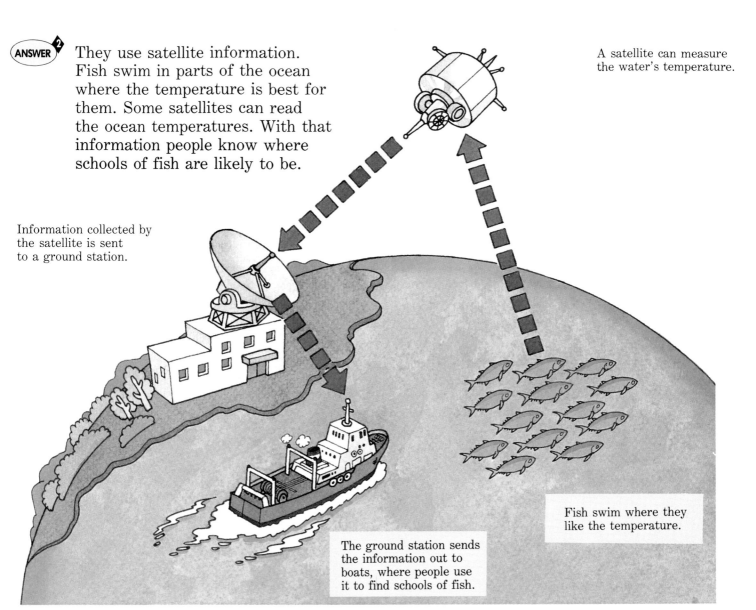

Fish swim where they like the temperature.

The ground station sends the information out to boats, where people use it to find schools of fish.

■ It can find fish near the surface

Fish live either close to the surface or near the bottom of the ocean. A satellite can detect only surface temperatures, so it can't help locate areas where there may be fish at the bottom of the ocean.

A satellite can keep track of fish that move from one area to another.

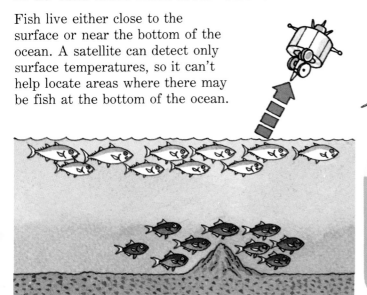

● **To the Parent**

A fishfinder operates in the same way as radar except that a radar set uses radio waves, while a fishfinder uses ultrasonic waves. These waves emitted from a fishing boat are easily reflected when they hit an object under the sea because they have a short wavelength. Sound waves with a longer wavelength, such as those employed in radar detection, cannot be used because that type of sound wave is not easily reflected beneath the surface of the water.

? Why Don't Birds Get Shocked When They Sit on an Electric Wire?

(ANSWER) If electricity passes through the body of a person or an animal it causes an electric shock. But when a bird is perched on a wire the current passes through the wire, not through the bird. That's why the bird doesn't get shocked.

■ A difference in voltage makes the current flow

Current flows because there is a difference in voltage between one end of the wire and the other. Similar to the way that water flows from a high place to a low one, electric current flows from high to low voltage. The voltage difference between an electric wire and the ground may be between 100 and several thousand volts. If anything provides a path between the wire and the ground, current will flow through it.

If electric current flows through a bird, it will be severely shocked.

If a bird perches on only one wire, the bird will not be hurt at all.

■ Why some birds are killed by wires

If a bird perches on two wires, or if its body touches an electric pole, a path is made for the current to flow between the two different voltages.

If a bird perches on two electric wires the current flows from one wire, through the bird, to the other.

If the bird touches an electric pole the current flows through the bird and pole to the ground.

How Does an Electric Shock Kill a Bird?

When an electric current passes through something, heat is produced. When a strong current flows through a bird or other animal it makes enough heat to cause a bad burn. The shock caused by the current can make the animal's heart stop. A powerful current can cause a very bad injury or even death, but a weak current usually isn't dangerous.

You must NEVER, NEVER touch any kind of electric wire!

● **To the Parent**

There are voltage differences between electric lines extending from one pole to another and between the power lines and the ground. A person on the ground receives an electric shock from touching one of the wires because the electric current flows through the person's body to the ground. A bird perched on a power line does not get a shock because current does not flow through its body.

❓ Why Does Food Spoil?

ANSWER When food gets old it spoils. That happens because there are tiny, invisible bacteria in the food. As the bacteria grow in number they use the food. They dissolve proteins and other substances in the food. When they do that we say the food is spoiled.

> When protein dissolves, it changes color and shape. It smells bad, too.

■ The food spoilers

Bacteria live on the nourishment they take from protein. They get it by breaking down or dissolving the protein.

Once protein is broken down by bacteria, it's no longer protein. It has changed, and it can't be eaten.

Why Does Spoiled Food Make Us Sick If We Eat It?

Too many bacteria in food cause it to spoil. If we eat the spoiled food we then have too many bacteria in our stomach, and that makes us feel sick. Another reason we get sick is that bacteria produce harmful substances in food, and those can upset our stomach.

Be sure not to eat food that's spoiled!

You'll get a stomachache if you eat things you shouldn't.

If you eat food with lots of bacteria you'll get sick.

Some bacteria are useful

Bacteria change things, and many of those changes are useful to us. To name one example, bacteria break down the ingredients of milk to make yogurt and cheese. And the vinegar that we use to make pickles is alcohol that bacteria have changed.

▲ Yogurt starts with milk, which is changed by the action of two kinds of bacteria that break it down. When bacteria break down alcohol, one of the results is vinegar, which is used to make salads and sauerkraut.

▲ Like yogurt, cheese starts with milk. It is broken down and changed by bacteria and then is pressed and shaped.

● **To the Parent**

Eating food that has gone bad because of the action of bacteria can cause illness. The bacteria consumed in the spoiled food multiply in the stomach and produce nausea. More serious is the food poisoning brought on by bacteria that give off poison as they are breaking down the food. Some bacterial action is beneficial, however, as in the fermentation processes for dairy and alcohol products.

Did You Know That a Diamond Is the Hardest Stone?

(ANSWER) Diamonds are made of carbon. The tiniest bits of carbon are called atoms. In a diamond, carbon atoms are held together in a special way. That's why it is so hard.

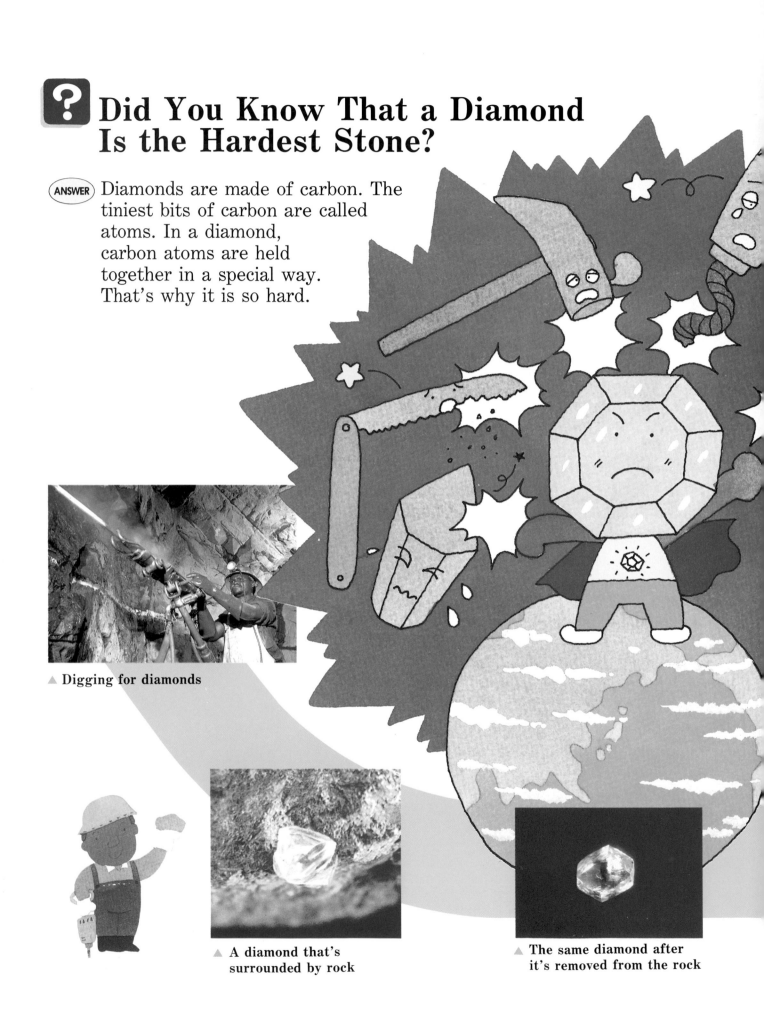

▲ Digging for diamonds

▲ A diamond that's surrounded by rock

▲ The same diamond after it's removed from the rock

● To the Parent

Both diamonds and the graphite in pencil lead are made of carbon atoms, but graphite is quite soft while diamonds are the hardest substance occurring in nature. The difference is in the way the atoms are bonded. The dense bonding of atoms into crystals in a diamond accounts for its hardness. Intense heat and pressure in the earth's interior are what change carbon into diamonds, the world's favorite gemstones.

■ How are diamonds and pencil lead related?

Diamonds and pencil lead both come from carbon.

■ How do they cut diamonds?

Diamonds are very hard, but they can be cut by using diamond powder.

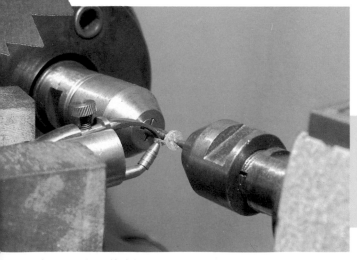

▲ Cutting and polishing a diamond on a machine

▲ A cut and polished diamond set in a ring

Why Doesn't the World Run Out of Oxygen?

(ANSWER) Plants produce oxygen. We won't run out of it or even run short of it as long as lots of green plants like trees and grass are growing.

Nature's balance

People and other animals take in oxygen and give off carbon dioxide. This is called breathing.

Plants take in carbon dioxide and give off oxygen. That's why we don't run short of oxygen.

■ What is photosynthesis?

Using energy from the sun, plants produce food from water and carbon dioxide. This is called photosynthesis, and it takes place in the green leaves of most plants. During photosynthesis oxygen is released.

Chloroplast

Oxygen

Carbon dioxide

Water

Will we ever run short of oxygen?

If too many trees are cut down it could reduce the supply of oxygen.

❓ Why Does Ice Float in Water?

ANSWER Like most substances, water is made up of many small particles called molecules. In water they are packed tightly together. The molecules in ice are not packed so tightly. Even though they take up more space they are lighter. Since ice is lighter than water, it floats.

▲ **An iceberg near the South Pole**

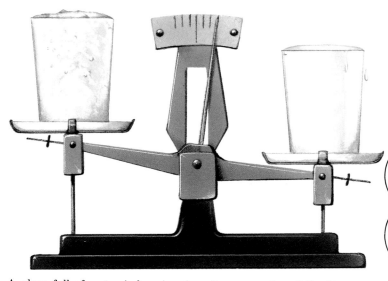

A glass full of water is heavier than the same glass full of ice.

Ice is lighter than water but not very much. About one eighth of an iceberg is above the surface of the ocean. The rest is below the surface.

■ Molecules in water and ice

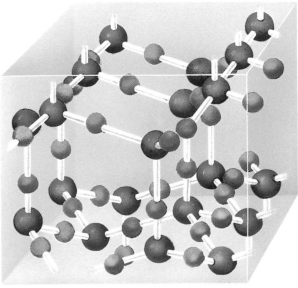

If ice turns to water the gaps will become much smaller.

If the water turns to ice the gaps will grow larger.

There are many gaps between molecules in ice.

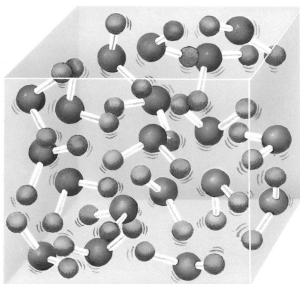

The molecules in water are packed tightly.

Put ice into a glass and then fill the glass with water. You can see that the ice rises above the top of the glass. Do you think the water will overflow when the ice melts? Try it and you'll find that it won't, because the number of molecules inside remains the same whether it's ice or water.

Fill the glass with water and freeze it. When all the water is frozen you'll see that the ice rises above the top of the glass. That happens because the amount of water increases if it freezes. When water turns into ice the amount increases by about 12%.

Did You Know That a Lake Freezes From the Top?

Water molecules are the most tightly packed together and the water is heaviest when it cools to 39° F. (3.9° C.), which is just above freezing. This heavier water sinks, leaving the water at the top of the lake to be exposed to freezing cold.

The top is frozen.

The water here still isn't frozen.

What is described here is what happens in a natural situation. There can be exceptions to this, but they would be extremely rare.

● To the Parent

When most substances are changed from a liquid state or gas to a solid state, the volume becomes smaller. But when water is turned into a solid in the form of ice its volume increases. This is because the hydrogen atoms of water molecules push apart from each other as the water turns from a liquid state into ice. Because the molecules in ice are less densely packed than the ones in water, ice floats.

❓ Why Doesn't Dry Ice Turn to Water The Way Regular Ice Does?

(ANSWER) Regular ice is made from water. When it melts it turns back into water. Dry ice is not made from water. Instead it is made from the gas called carbon dioxide. This gas is in the air around us. It is what dry ice turns into when it melts.

How molecules behave

Water changes to steam, which is a gas, when it is heated to 212° F. (100° C.) At 32° F. (0° C.) water changes to ice, which is its solid form. So we say that water has three states.

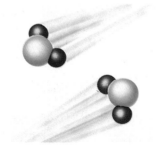

Water molecules as gas

Under pressure carbon dioxide can be changed from a gas into a solid. When that happens it becomes dry ice. Under very high pressure carbon dioxide can be turned into a liquid.

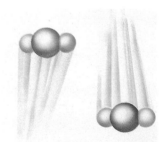

Carbon dioxide as gas

Water molecules as liquid

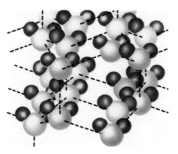

Water molecules as ice

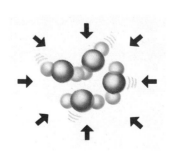

Carbon dioxide as liquid

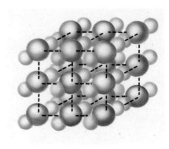

Carbon dioxide as a solid

How Is Dry Ice Made?

Carbon dioxide gas is put under extremely high pressure and then cooled to -4° F. (-20° C.). That turns the gas into a liquid. Then the pressure is immediately reduced to normal air pressure. The liquid instantly turns to gas. This also causes a sharp reduction in temperature. That turns some of the gas into something that looks like snow. This is pressed together into blocks of dry ice.

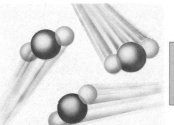

Carbon dioxide gas

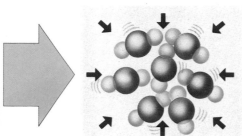

Pressure and cooling turn it into a liquid.

The pressure is decreased.

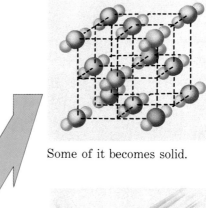

Some of it becomes solid.

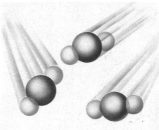

Some becomes a gas again.

People who handle dry ice wear gloves to protect their skin.

MINI-DATA

When dry ice is put into a glass of water it bubbles as the carbon dioxide becomes a gas.

When dry ice is put into water with detergent in it it makes soap bubbles of carbon dioxide.

How Is Uranium Used To Make Electricity?

ANSWER At a nuclear power plant atoms are split in two, and that releases a lot of heat. This heat is then used in the plant's nuclear power generator to produce electricity.

A nuclear reactor has a pale glow.

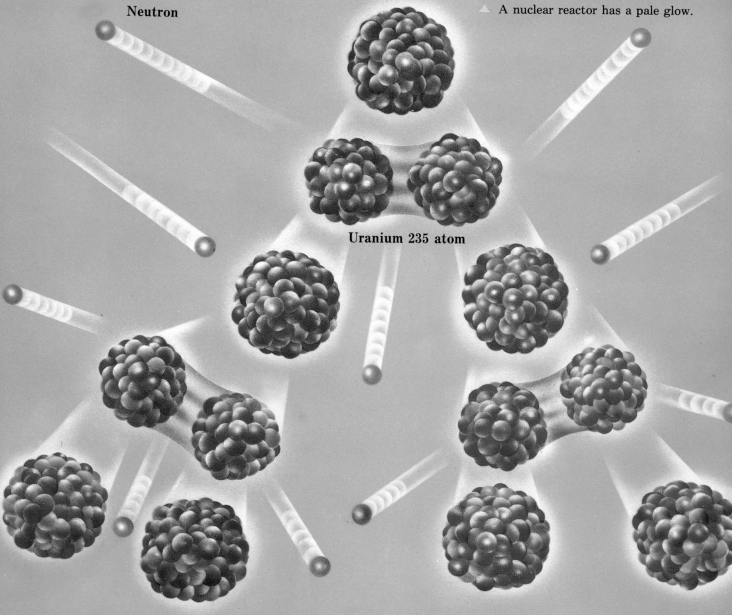

Neutron

Uranium 235 atom

Inside a Nuclear Power Plant

Heat generated inside the reactor makes water
circulating around it boil and produce steam.
The steam turns turbines to make electricity.

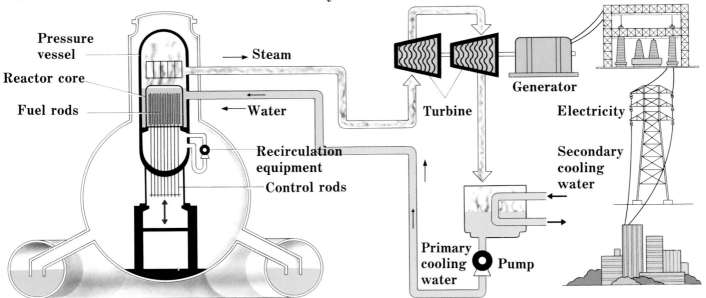

A lot of energy from a little fuel

Nuclear power produces a lot of energy from a small
amount of fuel. Splitting the atoms in one tiny bit of
uranium can give us the same amount of energy as we
would get from burning huge amounts of oil or coal.

Uranium
1/28 ounce
(1 g)

Oil
530
gallons
(2,000 l)

It takes this much oil to produce the same energy.

The energy from 1/28 ounce (1 g)
of uranium will run 23,000
television sets for one hour.

A small car could
go halfway around
the world on 1/28 ounce
(1 g) of uranium.

Uranium
1/28 ounce
(1 g)

Coal
3⅓
tons
(3 t)

It takes this much coal to produce the same energy.

? How Do Farmers Grow Seedless Grapes?

ANSWER Two weeks before flowers appear on the vines the buds are dipped in a special liquid. The liquid contains a special substance that comes from a fungus. Ten days after the flowers bloom they are dipped again. That is what causes the grapes to be seedless.

▲ Grape buds are dipped in this liquid.

■ The fungus does it

If grape buds are not soaked in a special solution, the grapes will have seeds in them.

If grape buds are soaked in this special solution, seedless grapes are formed.

▲ **Grapes with seeds**

Buds are soaked before blooming.   They're soaked again after they bloom.

▲ **Seedless grapes**

Are Seedless Watermelons Grown the Same Way?

It's done a different way. All living things, even watermelons, have chromosomes. If we mix watermelons with different chromosomes we get seedless ones.

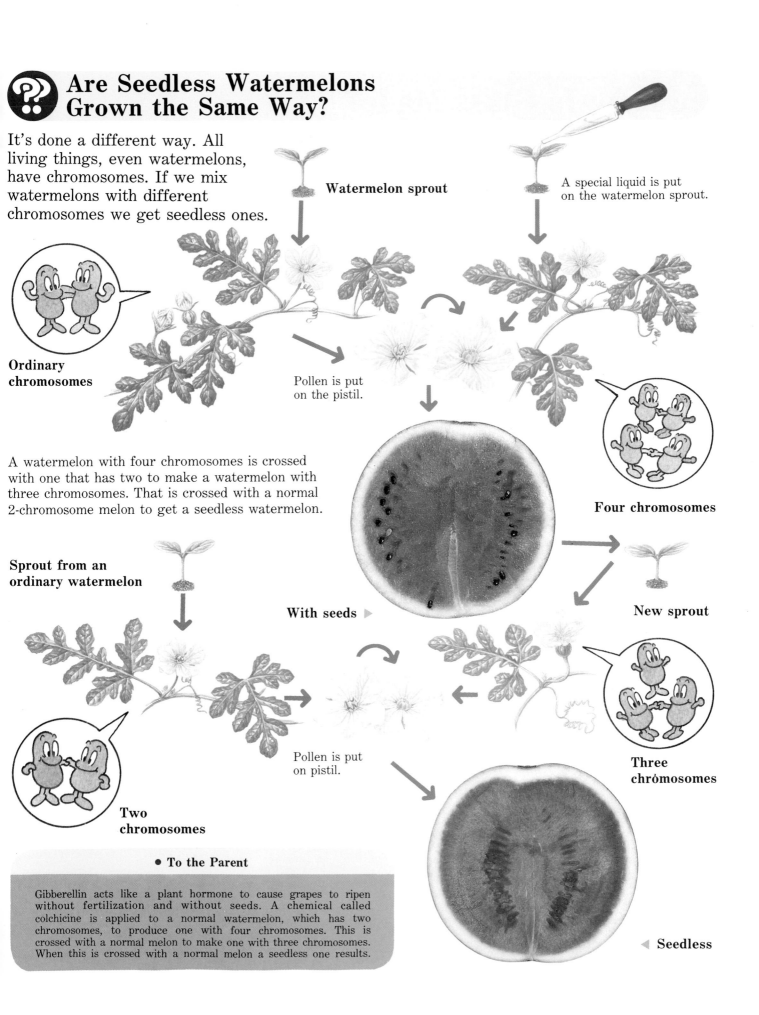

Watermelon sprout

A special liquid is put on the watermelon sprout.

Ordinary chromosomes

Pollen is put on the pistil.

A watermelon with four chromosomes is crossed with one that has two to make a watermelon with three chromosomes. That is crossed with a normal 2-chromosome melon to get a seedless watermelon.

Four chromosomes

With seeds ▶

New sprout

Sprout from an ordinary watermelon

Pollen is put on pistil.

Three chromosomes

Two chromosomes

• To the Parent

Gibberellin acts like a plant hormone to cause grapes to ripen without fertilization and without seeds. A chemical called colchicine is applied to a normal watermelon, which has two chromosomes, to produce one with four chromosomes. This is crossed with a normal melon to make one with three chromosomes. When this is crossed with a normal melon a seedless one results.

◀ Seedless

💡 How Is Glass Made?

(ANSWER) Glass is made from silica, soda ash and limestone. When it is heated, the mixture of minerals melts and forms molten glass. The soft, hot glass is shaped and then cooled. Many things are made of glass by machines. But artists called glass blowers make pretty objects like vases by blowing into molten glass on a long tube.

▲ Beautiful shapes of glass

■ Plate glass made by rolling

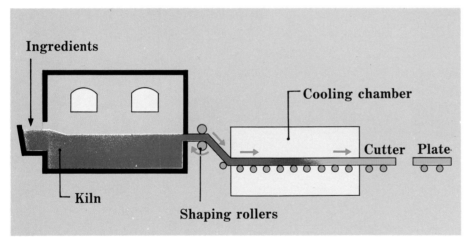

Ingredients

Cooling chamber

Cutter Plate

Kiln

Shaping rollers

The ingredients are heated in a kiln to make molten glass. Rollers flatten the glass into sheets, which are cooled and cut into pieces.

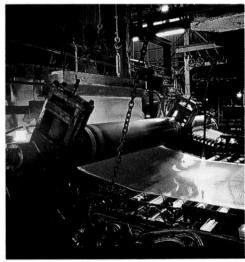

▲ **Rolling process.** Rollers press the molten glass into sheets to be cut.

■ Plate glass made by floating

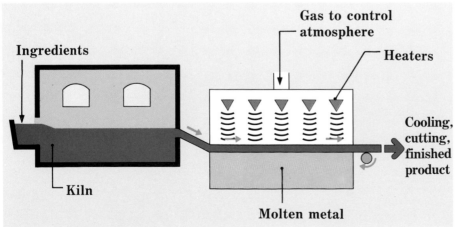

Gas to control atmosphere

Ingredients

Heaters

Cooling, cutting, finished product

Kiln

Molten metal

Molten glass from the kiln is floated and slowly cooled in a bath of molten metal. After the glass cools down it's cut into pieces.

▲ **Float-bath process.** Molten glass cools as it floats on a bath of molten metal.

Handmade Glassware

Vases, tiny figures of animals and other glass objects are made one at a time by glass blowing. Using a metal blowpipe with a glob of molten glass at the end of it, the artist blows the soft glass into the desired shape.

▲ The raw materials are heated so that they turn into molten glass.

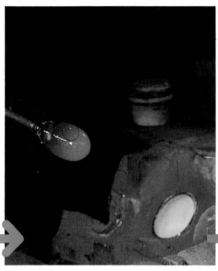

▲ A glob of molten glass is wound around the end of the blowpipe.

▲ While blowing on the pipe the glass blower turns it to shape the object.

Glass has many uses

Window panes, mirrors and drinking glasses are just a few of the many things in our daily life that are made of glass. And glass is not only useful, it can be beautiful. Windows made of colored, or stained, glass are works of art.

▲ **Stained glass windows in a church**

⁇ What Are These?

■ A waterfall

A waterfall is a steep descent of water to a lower height. The highest waterfall in the world is Angel Falls in Venezuela. There the water falls 3,212 feet (979 m). A waterfall is sometimes called a cataract, especially if it has a large volume of water. A series of smaller waterfalls is called a cascade.

■ A U-shaped valley

Most valleys are V-shaped. But some are U-shaped like the one in this picture. U-shaped valleys were formed thousands of years ago as glaciers moved through, grinding away rocks and earth.

Look! That valley was run over by a glacier!

■ Karst

A karst is an area that has a lot of limestone near the surface of the ground. Because limestone is easily dissolved by rainwater, a karstic area has lots of caves, sinkholes and underground streams that have been cut into the rock by the water. The surface of the ground is rocky and has almost no trees or grass growing on it.

■ A corona

The light that we sometimes can see around the sun is called a corona. It's the sun's atmosphere. We usually can't see the corona because the sun's light is so bright. But when the moon blocks the sun's brightness in a solar eclipse we can see the corona's beautiful pearl-gray light.

■ An observatory

In an observatory there's a large telescope. Scientists called astronomers use it to observe the stars and other objects in the sky. The observatory's dome can be turned in a full circle, in whatever direction the telescope needs to be pointed. The dome opens so astronomers can look into the sky with the telescope.

■ A crater on the moon

These craters were formed by meteorites that crashed into the moon. One reason we don't see craters like this on earth is that meteorites usually burn up before they reach the ground. Friction with the air in our atmosphere causes them to burn up. But the moon has no atmosphere, so meteorites crash into it at high speeds and dig out large craters like this.

● **To the Parent**

Karstic regions have large deposits of limestone that are eroded by rain and wind. They are characterized by barren surfaces, caves and sinkholes. The term was first applied to a region near Trieste called Karst. The corona is the sun's atmosphere of high-temperature gases. It is visible only during a solar eclipse, when the moon prevents us from seeing the rest of the sun.

❓ And What Are These?

■ The Milky Way

The Milky Way is a large group of stars. Our earth and sun are part of the Milky Way, and sometimes we speak of it as our galaxy. There are many galaxies like this in the universe. The Milky Way is known as a spiral galaxy because it looks like a spiraling patch of clouds. Actually it's made up of thousands of stars like our sun.

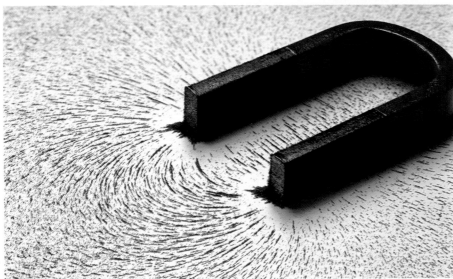

■ Magnetic lines of force

You can't see them, but there are magnetic lines of force around any magnet. You can see the effect of that force if you put a magnet on a piece of paper and sprinkle iron filings around it. The lines of force will make the tiny pieces of iron form curved patterns like the ones shown in this photograph.

■ An astronaut walking in space

A spaceship in orbit is in a state of weightlessness, and so is anything outside the spaceship. The astronaut and the spaceship are orbiting the earth at the same speed. That's why the astronaut doesn't fall but instead stays close to the spaceship.

Growing-Up Album

How Are They Related? 82
Which Shadows Match? 84
How Do They Differ? 86

How Are They Related?

The boys and girls shown here are doing things or are involved in situations that are related somehow to the objects at the bottom of these two pages. Can you figure out what that relationship is? Think about it, then match the objects below with the boys' and girls' actions and situations above.

1. It's raining.

2. He's swimming underwater.

3. They're looking at the stars.

4. They're ice skating.

■ What's the connection?

These 10 objects have something to do with the situations and actions that you see in the pictures above. Think about how they're related.

A golf ball   **Compressed air**   **Ice**   **Glass**   **The sun**

5. There are shadows on the ground.

6. They're figuring out which way to go.

7. She's playing golf.

8. He can see outside even though the window is closed.

9. She can eat her ice cream because it hasn't melted.

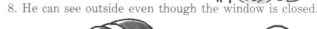

10. She's playing tennis.

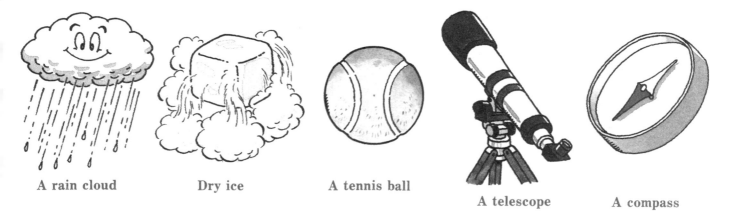

A rain cloud   **Dry ice**   **A tennis ball**   **A telescope**   **A compass**

83

1. A rain cloud 2. Compressed air 3. A telescope 4. Ice 5. The sun 6. A compass 7. A golf ball 8. Glass 9. Dry ice 10. A tennis ball

Which Shadows Match?

When the sun shines on a person or object it casts a shadow. In this picture you can see a lot of shadows. At the bottom are six more shadows. Look at them carefully, then match the shadows at the bottom with the people, animals or objects that made them.

■ Match the Shadows

These six shadows can be found in the picture above. Some of the shadows in the picture are similar, so look very carefully. For each one of these six shadows, there's only one exactly like it in the picture. Can you find it?

①

②

③

④ ⑤ ⑥

1. Light-colored car on the right 2. Dog in the park 3. Boy on the right in the park
4. Boy carrying package on bicycle 5. Woman with baby carriage 6. Tree that's closest to you

How Do They Differ?

There is water both in rivers and in the sea, but they are different in many ways. Try to find the differences.

■ What are the differences?

Pictures 1 through 8 at right show things that might be either in the sea or in a river. Words below them will help you guess where each is being done. Can you guess which ones are in a river and which ones are in the sea?

1. It can be held back by a dam.

2. It tastes salty.

3. It can create a waterfall.

4. Its current always flows the same way.

5. It sometimes
has big waves.

6. It has a tide.

7. You often paddle
a canoe there.

8. You can surf on it.

A river: 1,3,4,7 The sea: 2,5,6,8

A Child's First Library of Learning

Science Starter

Time-Life Books Inc. is a wholly owned subsidiary of
The Time Inc. Book Company
Time-Life Books, Alexandria, Virginia
Children's Publishing

Publisher:	Robert H. Smith
Editorial Director:	Neil Kagan
Associate Editor:	Jean Burke Crawford
Marketing Director:	Ruth P. Stevens
Promotion Director:	Kathleen B. Tresnak
Associate Promotion Director:	Jane B. Welihozkiy
Production Manager:	Prudence G. Harris
Editorial Consultants:	Jacqueline A. Ball
	Andrew Gutelle

Editorial Supervision by:
International Editorial Services Inc.
Tokyo, Japan

Editor:	C. E. Berry
Associate Editor:	Winston S. Priest
Translation:	Joseph Hlebica
	Bryan Harrell
Writer:	Pauline Bush
Editorial Staff:	Christine Alaimo
	Nobuko Abe

Cover:	Courtesy of NASA

TIME LIFE ®

Library of Congress Cataloging in Publication Data
Science starter.
     p.   cm.—(A Child's first library of learning)
   Summary: Questions and answers provide information
about what a mirage is, why milk turns sour, how a lunar
eclipse occurs, and other scientific phenomena. Includes charts,
diagrams, and an activities section.
   ISBN 0-8094-4881-5.   ISBN 0-8094-4882-3 (lib. bdg.)
   1. Science—Miscellanea—Juvenile literature.   [1.
Science—Miscellanea.   2. Questions and answers.]
I. Time-Life Books.   II. Series.
Q163.S468   1989   500—dc20   89-4534
©1989 Time-Life Books Inc.
©1988 Gakken Co. Ltd.

Second printing 1991. Printed in U.S.A.
Published simultaneously in Canada.

TIME-LIFE is a trademark of Time Warner Inc. U.S.A.

Time-Life Books Inc. offers a wide range of fine publications,
including home video products. For subscription information,
call 1-800-621-7026 or write TIME-LIFE BOOKS, P.O. Box
C-32068, Richmond, Virginia 23261-2068.